TEN MEN

TEN MEN

Examining the Passion and Progress of
Black Men on Charlotte's Historic West Side

Copyright 2017

ISBN: 978-0-9916393-3-5

Printed in the U.S.A.
Production manager: Keisha Talbot Johnson
Managing editor: Angela Vogel Daley
Designer: Christine Long
Photo editor: Wendy Yang
Illustrator: Jerry McJunkins

The contents of this Smith Institute for Applied Research publication were developed under the Title III Student Aid and Fiscal Responsibility Act (SAFRA), Award Number P031B150062, from the Department of Education. However, the contents do not necessarily represent the policy of the Department of Education, and you should not assume endorsement by the Federal Government.

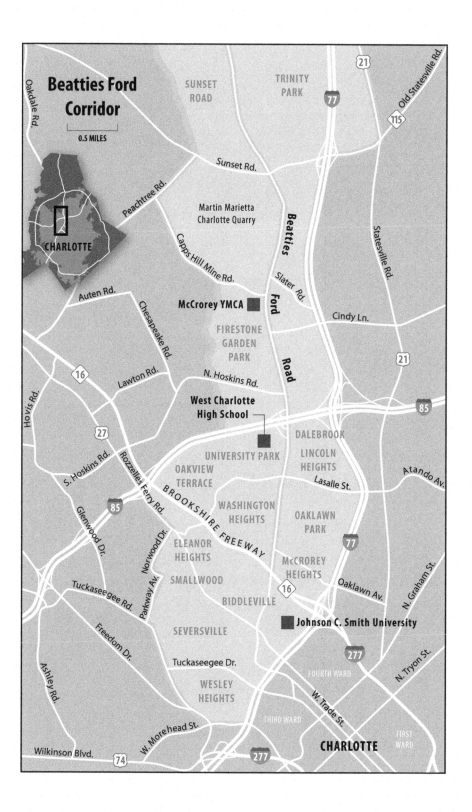

TABLE OF CONTENTS

Acknowledgements ix

Preface, Dr. Ronald L. Carter xi

Foreword, Dr. Jonathan N. Livingston xv

Introduction, Ron Stodghill xix

Charles Jones 01

Colin Pinkney 13

Justin Harlow 23

Damian Johnson 33

Melvin Herring 45

Darrel Williams 55

Titus Ivory 65

Jerry McJunkins 79

Alvin Austin 91

Darryl Gaston 99

The West End, Tiffany Taylor 111

Epilogue, Dr. Diane Bowles 113

About the Editor 119

ACKNOWLEDGEMENTS

I would like to express my sincerest gratitude to the numerous individuals who contributed to this book, through their moral or financial support, their academic research or personal recollections, or their editorial or administrative efforts. I would especially like to thank Dr. Ronald L. Carter, President of Johnson C. Smith University, for his passion, vision, and stewardship of this project; and Dr. Diane Bowles, University Vice President and Executive Director of the Smith Institute for Applied Research, for her generosity in funding the work; and Dr. Brian Jones, Dean of College of Arts and Letters, and Dr. Erin DiCesare, Chair of Interdisciplinary Studies, for their support.

I'd also like to thank my terrific editorial team: managing editor Angela Vogel Daley, designer Christine Long, photo editor Wendy Yang, sketch artist Jerry McJunkins, map artist Bill Pitzer, production manager Keisha Talbot Johnson, and administrator Margaret Watson. Many thanks to Latrelle McAllister, JCSU's Executive Director of Human Resources, for granting us permission to publish her late father, James Peeler's, extraordinary photographs; as well as Monika Rhue, Brandon Lunsford, and photo archivist Chelly Tavss for their assistance in preparing Mr. Peeler's collection for print. Much gratitude also to the many who invested time and research into the numerous other images within the photo insert, including Todd Sumlin, Diedra Laird, Maria David, Shelia Bumgarner, Tom Cole, Tyrus Ortega Gaines, John D. Simmons, Sherry Waters, and T'Afo Feimster. Also, I appreciate all those individuals who helped identify and offered insight into the people and places shaping Charlotte's West Side, especially Mattie Marshall, President of Washington Heights Community Association, Inc., and Alysia D. Osborne, Director of Historic West End with Charlotte Center City Partners.

And thank you always to God from whom all blessings flow.

R.S.

PREFACE

By Dr. Ronald L. Carter

P erhaps I can best explain the aim of this book as follows. During my life and times here in Charlotte I have heard conversations, read reports, and debated recommendations about black men that always seem to start from a deficit perspective. The focus is on their deficits—problems and pathologies within their family and circumstances. This approach concerns me because it too often overlooks, even marginalizes, the strengths and resources of the individual that help him or her live with problems he or she faces from day to day as a thinker and doer. I am equally concerned that the context for deficit problem-solving is, as it must be, rooted in cultural and belief systems that may not be diverse and inclusive enough to do justice to the aspects, sense data, values, intuitions, and hopes that make experience meaningful. And, I am always mindful of Ludwig Wittgenstein's observation in his *Philosophy of Investigations* that there are "countless different kinds of use of what we call 'symbols,' 'words,' 'sentences.'" With all the aforementioned in mind, I am very cautious when it comes to focusing primarily on deficit perspectives of "the black male," because they can easily be misinterpreted given their complexities and can unwittingly get lost in barren and misleading illusions about black men.

Let me hasten to say here that I am not pushing for a "Pollyanna view" of the black male. Even though there is some evidence that the brain is hard-wired for optimism, unrealistic optimism can be even more dangerous than deficit problem-solving. There are indeed issues, challenges, and problems that stifle the voice, choice, and development of black men. And this book addresses some of the challenges in the section on the demographic profile of West Side men and throughout the views of the men represented in this work. What I am pressing for are both a strengths-based and melioristic view of black men.

Since I am often described as a "wannabe social worker," let me turn to a very brief description of the strengths perspective in social work theory and practice. Prior to the 1990s, social workers' approach to individual and family case management started with the assumption that their clients become clients because they have deficits and were flawed or weak. But the question emerges: is this a "solution-caused problem"? In other words, does the deficit/problem-based model lead to much bigger problems? Dennis Saleebey thinks it does and succinctly sums it with these words: "Focusing on problems usually creates more problems. The longer one stays with a problem-focused assessment, the more likely it is that the problem will dominate the scene." An alternative view, he and other social theorists argued, is to begin with the strengths, talents, resources, and assets of the individual and his/her family. This is not to ignore problems and dysfunctions, but the strengths-based approach encourages the individual to recognize and act on his or her strengths in order to offset weaknesses. In short, the individual, in collaboration with a social worker, empowers him or her to health and well-being. A strengths perspective of the black man would assume that he can find a way to live and learn on his empowering edge in whatever course he chooses to undertake because he understands and acts on the strengths of his capacities and aspirations and accordingly weaknesses are offset by strengths. This is empowerment at its best.

This leads to me to the notion of meliorism, which is the belief that human beings have an inherent tendency toward progress or improvement, that is to say, a prevailing disposition to move toward concerted human effort and interference to produce an improvement in the human condition. Individuals and families, small groups, organizations and communities, cities, states, and countries thrive by ameliorating conditions that cause suffering, by co-creating new realities out of stagnant circumstances, and even by the call of great ideas defined as inalienable rights. Accordingly, a melioristic view of black men would accordingly focus on the talents, capacities, skills, and watershed ideas of black men to improve their lives and communities. In short, a melioristic view would focus on the black man as an agent of change.

Thus, in commissioning this book, I wanted to approach the question, "Who are the West Side black men?" from a strengths-based perspective. Ten black men, speaking individually, present their philosophies about other black men who move and have their being on Charlotte's West Side. Their notions about reality, the nature of things, the meaning and outcome of life on the West Side are spoken with passionate insights that emerge from immersing themselves in the kindred activities of the community. The Burkinabe ritual teacher Sobonfu Somé has an insight that aptly captures the point I am pressing: "Go deep into your heart and listen to the rhythm of it. There is a language spoken to you by the beings you have called into your circle. The problem is, we usually don't listen enough, and therefore we don't hear it." The ten men in this book have gone deep into the heart of the matter concerning themselves as black men and their relationships with other West Side black men. They are skilled in listening and active in creating better ways of communicating about the black male. Each of these ten speaks from a strengths-based perspective, as noted in a preface to their remarks.

The end question of this book is whether or not the perspectives of the ten men are representative of West Side black men. If so, how can we incorporate this representation in our narratives and research about black men? And if not, can we learn from these ten black men better ways to listen to the voice of the West Side black male? My colleague, Dr. Diane Bowles, makes suggestions in the Epilogue about future research opportunities around these two questions.

I challenge the reader to approach this work with an open mind, to "listen to the rhythm" of the conversation that seeks to create new realities about West Side black men and perhaps black men everywhere.

Dr. Ronald L. Carter is the 13th president of Johnson C. Smith University.

FOREWORD

By Dr. Jonathan N. Livingston and Jasmine B. Bethea

**"I don't want to grow up as black man
in Charlotte because you can get killed."**

*8-year-old black boy at Charlotte City
Council meeting after the 2016 riots*

In late September 2016, as riots erupted in the heart of Charlotte, the city many affectionately regard as the "hub of the New South," found itself under a harsh national spotlight. The fatal shooting of another black male by police officers attracted major media and the National Guard—while also affirming long-held predictions that local police brutality, racial provocations, and economic inequities would one day explode in civil unrest.

As days of riots and mayhem followed the seemingly unjust shooting, city leaders struggled to understand the historical and economic factors that led to the riots and created the conditions that many black men experience in Charlotte. Indeed, if Charlotte's rise as among the top banking centers in the country has made it one of the nation's fastest-growing cities, its affluence has been mostly confined to the southern parts of town. As a result, the median income for families on the city's West Side has been statistically lower than other areas of Charlotte, along with the median price of homes and rates of home ownership.

Of course, Charlotte's narrative of black underachievement and pathology has been well chronicled: stories of substandard housing where a disproportionate number of the residents receive government assistance, tales about the influx of crack cocaine in the 1980s, an intergenerational vicious cycle of violence and poverty consuming the West Side, sagas of two generations of children born within a nexus of unmet educational and economic needs, all of which have contributed to higher rates of high school dropouts, violence, incarceration, poverty, homelessness, and unemployment.

But this book, edited by award-winning journalist Ron Stodghill, an assistant professor at Johnson C. Smith University, explores through a series of interviews the rarely told narrative of Charlotte's black men as survivors, as community leaders, as agents of change. In the 1960s and '70s, for example, as Charlotte experienced some of the most heated racial tensions in the country over the issue of bussing, what became of the many black male youth on the West Side who were bussed to schools in South Charlotte and East Charlotte in an effort to ensure racial equity in the school district? Despite daily harassment and abuse from students and teachers alike, many went on to graduate high school and attend colleges, while others dropped out to become skilled laborers or work in the service industry downtown to build families and community. Following the 1970s and the Vietnam War, as many West Side neighborhoods saw a substantial increase of heroin use and crime, and in the 1980s, as crack cocaine devastated their West Side communities and caused outward migrations of whites as well as the black middle-class, many black men stayed behind to work as educators, pastors, coaches, and community volunteers.

These men, many of whom are natives of Charlotte, are central to any col-

FOREWORD

lective understanding of Charlotte's history and future. They helped build
the skyline, buildings, and arenas that many enjoy in Charlotte today; they
are the truck drivers, waiters, cooks, barbers, bus drivers, construction workers, educators, and fathers—and their experiences have been largely untold
or undervalued. Yet these men prevail. Living an existentialist life, African-American men on the West Side of Charlotte have always understood
clearly that life is indeed what you make it.

*Dr. Jonathan N. Livingston is a Senior Research Fellow for Johnson C. Smith
University's Smith Institute for Applied Research. He is also an Associate Professor at North Carolina Central University's Department of Psychology.*

*Jasmine B. Bethea is a senior at North Carolina Central University majoring
in psychology.*

INTRODUCTION

By Ron Stodghill

Some sixty-five years have passed since Ralph Ellison depicted in his novel *Invisible Man* the surreal and tragic paradox of being born with dark skin in America. As Ellison's unnamed protagonist opens in the 1952 classic: "I am a man of substance, of flesh and bone, fiber and liquids—and I might even be said to possess a mind. I am invisible, understand, simply because people refuse to see me. Like the bodiless heads you see sometimes in circus sideshows, it is as though I have been surrounded by mirrors of hard, distorting glass. When they approach me they see only my surroundings, themselves, or figments of their imagination ..."

While Ellison's masterpiece is set between the South in the 1920s and 1930s Harlem, his portrayal of black disillusionment, isolation, and frustration have unfortunately proven a timeless state of being—through subsequent decades of human rights rhetoric and anti-discrimination policy initiatives. In fact, the rioting that gripped Charlotte in 2016 seemed an eerie epilogue to Ellison's fiction—as hundreds of black men protested the police shooting and death of forty-three-year-year-old Charlotte resident Keith Lamont Scott. The three-day protests drew international news coverage, as mobs engulfed by tear gas—some shattering storefront windows and looting—resulted in then-Governor Pat McCrory declaring a state of emergency and deploying the National Guard. Reminiscent of similar uprisings in such cities as Ferguson, Missouri, and Baltimore, Maryland, Charlotte's riots cast President Obama in the awkward position of denouncing the rioters themselves while empathizing with their urge to riot. "I think it's important to separate out the pervasive sense of frustration among a lot of African Americans about the shootings of people and the sense that justice is not always color blind," he said.

Indeed, across the board, from classrooms to prisons, the nation's racial inequities remain staggering—decades after the passage of landmark Civil Rights Acts in 1957 and 1964, which granted African Americans voting rights, and, respectively, banned workplace and hiring discrimination based on race and gender. Today, one in three black men can expect to go to prison in their lifetime, incarcerated at nearly six times the rate of whites, according to the Bureau of Justice Statistics. This is especially startling considering that African Americans account for some 13% of the U.S. population compared to Whites, who make up 77%. The result is some 1.5 million black men have disappeared from the American landscape, *The New York Times* estimated in its sweeping 2015 report on black male criminal injustice. "In New York, almost 120,000 black men between the ages of twenty-five and fifty-four are missing from everyday life. In Chicago, 45,000 are, and more than 30,000 are missing from Philadelphia. Across the South—from North Charleston, S.C., through Georgia, Alabama, Mississippi, and up into Ferguson, Mo.—hundreds of thousands are missing. They are missing because of early deaths or because they are behind bars."

Ten Men: Examining the Passion and Progress of Black Men on Charlotte's Historic West Side is a literary antidote to these sobering statistics. An oral

INTRODUCTION

history featuring ten high-impact local African-American men connected through birth or service to one of Charlotte's oldest African-American communities, *Ten Men* hopes to restore voice to the voiceless, distinction to the discarded with wisdom, candor, and insight. In this work, readers are invited into the minds and hearts of some of the most dynamic change agents as they work through neighborhood associations, book clubs, classrooms, churches, gymnasiums, and barbershops. As Ronald L. Carter, president of Johnson C. Smith University, says, "These men are achieving at their growing edge."

To be sure, the literary canon is rich with anthologies on the black American experience, spanning Alain Locke's 1925 classic *The New Negro* to Terry McMillan's acclaimed *Breaking Ice*, published in 1990. In 1996, scholars Herb Boyd and Robert L. Allen broke new ground with *Brotherman: The Odyssey of Black Men in America*, the first anthology devoted exclusively to African-American male authors. A voluminous work, *Brotherman* features an array of classic and contemporary voices from Charles Chestnut, W.E.B. Du Bois, and Paul Robeson, to Ellis Cose, Ice-T, and Henry Louis Gates, Jr. In *Brotherman*, Boyd and Allen sought to "create a living mosaic of essays and stories in which black men can view themselves and be viewed without distortion."

Ten Men boasts similar aspirations, albeit through narrative accounts that are intentionally first-person, hyper-local, and largely prescriptive. This book is set squarely on Charlotte's West Side, an area undergoing dramatic change, with a steady migration of a diverse mix of black and white affluent homeowners, an imminent Gold Line streetcar, and new business and commercial construction that is reshaping one of Charlotte's historically African-American communities. As local historian Dr. Dan Morrill puts it: "As the trade path and setting for transformational events in Charlotte's history and the birthplace of Charlotte's Civil Rights movement, the Historic West End has been rightly called 'the most historic place in Charlotte.'"

As local policymakers and community leaders grapple with the area's future, the views and concerns of black men—who, along with black women, comprise the Historic West End's most critical demographic—are often drowned out, erased, or relegated to terse TV news sound bites. Over several months in 2016 and 2017, I spent hours researching and interviewing several black men who are deeply connected and committed to the area and its future, as activists, educators, and spiritual and political leaders. Those conversations, taped and edited for length and clarity, form the essence of *Ten Men*, which casts black men through deed and symbolism in their rightful place at the heart of Charlotte's West Side.

Ten Men is also rooted in the intellectual tradition of historian and author Studs Terkel's 1974 classic *Working*, a hefty volume of transcribed confessions of average working Americans whose message ultimately transcends the book's mundane pretense. Terkel explains in *Working* that, beyond providing a window into Americans' often dispiriting grind to pay the bills, the oral histories are also "about a search, too, for daily meaning … for recognition as well as cash, for astonishment rather than torpor; in short, for a sort of life rather than a Monday through Friday sort of dying. Perhaps immortality, too, is part of the quest. To be remembered was the wish, spoken and unspoken, of the heroes and heroines of this book."

Of course, against the muted, marginalized history of black men in America, *Ten Men* is but a modest step in giving these local brothers a platform to be heard—or better yet, understood. As Ellison's unnamed protagonist laments: "You ache with the need to convince yourself that you do exist in the real world, that you're a part of all the sound and anguish, and you strike out with your fists, you curse and you swear to make them recognize you. And, alas, it's seldom successful." In these pages, our recognition is full and forever.

Ron Stodghill is an assistant professor of Interdisciplinary Studies at Johnson C. Smith University.

CHARLES JONES

Charles Jones is a Charlotte icon, a Freedom Rider during the Civil Rights Movement, and a longtime champion for residents and communities on the city's long-neglected West Side. A graduate of Johnson C. Smith University and Howard University Law School, Jones led several local protects in the 1960s, was involved in sit-in attempts across the South, and organized the SNCC at Shaw University in 1960. An attorney, Jones served as chair of the SNCC's direct action committee. He was one of the Rock Hill, South Carolina, Four. As a Freedom Rider, traveling on a Greyhound bus in May 1961 from Atlanta to Birmingham, he was arrested in Montgomery, Alabama. His work with such activists as Charles Sherrod, Cordell Reagon, and the Albany Movement landed him in jail on two occasions with Dr. Martin Luther King, Jr.

TEN MEN

I was born August 23, 1937, 4:30 in the mornin' down in Chester, South Carolina. And I said, "A'ight, world, let's do this." My sister, she thought I was a cat when I came out. Back then black folks were not admitted to hospitals except in an emergency. Dr. Allen lived about five blocks from where we lived in Chester, right across from Brainerd Institute, and he came to the house, pulled me out.

In November 1948, we moved from Chester to Charlotte to 2112 West Trade. This was called Biddleville. Everything on this side of Trade was Biddleville, for Biddle Hall, and all the black people lived here. Everything on the other side was Smallwood, where white folks lived.

There was no socializing at all between the two communities, except as kids. I was like nine or ten. All the houses on the other side were on the next street in front—these were the back of the houses. All the houses on this side, Biddleville, had front lawns on Trade. I remember the white kids would sometimes pick up pecans and throw them over and laugh and we'd pick 'em up and throw them back over and laugh and that was our way of communicating, literally. We were innocent kids.

My grandma on my mother's side lived in a little town called Irmo, about twelve miles from Columbia. She'd say, "Boy, you God's child. Don't nobody tell you you're less than anybody else but don't you start thinking you better because I'll smack you upside the back of yo' head. Now you go ahead and go as far as you want to and I always got your back."

My father, J.T. Jones, went to Johnson C. Smith and graduated. He and four of his brothers graduated from the Theologic Seminary. One of his brothers also was a dentist and went down to Macon, Georgia. These were men who stood tall, were well-respected, so that was the context. My background set for me a tone that legitimized my inherent self-dignity but also balanced it out. So that was the journey that I was walking with and through.

CHARLES JONES

We moved up here in '48. I went to West Charlotte High School where I graduated. I played alto saxophone in the band. I remember the West Charlotte band was invited to be the first African-American band in the Christmas parade, which went down Tryon Street and, at the Square as they do now, the bands would stop and perform. All the older black men pulled the young males in that band to the side and said, "First of all, we're proud of you. We know how you perform, you'll do very well. But we also want you to understand that the fathers, grandfathers of those white girls, majorettes and all, gonna be checking out whatever y'all lookin' at, doin', so be proud to do what you do, but don't let nobody see you staring at them young white majorettes."

And that was a critical moment because it was a point where it was clearly understood that they had our backs, but also this is a strange world we lived in. At the Square, we put it on, bro! There was a moment later where the band members, kind of laughing, said, "I remember what they warned us about, but did you all see that one girl? She didn't have hardly anything on, and she was doin' like we dance sometimes!" We laughed. That's a memory from that period in time.

* * * * * *

On February 1, 1960, I was driving back from Washington and I heard it broadcast about three or four in the morning: "Today, four young African-American students from A&T went down to Woolworth's in Greensboro, non-violently sat and vowed to continue to come back until they were served and treated like everybody else." And I said, "Yes! That's ... my generation, yo! Let's do this, let's rock and roll." I was a student at Smith and had been vice president of the student council, so when I got back to campus I gathered some of the leaders and I said, "Did y'all hear what happened up in Greensboro yesterday? Well, these students went down to Woolworth's, dignified, dressed appropriately and said they were gonna continue to come back until Woolworth's and all of the drug counters in the center city would open up and serve them like everybody else. I don't know about y'all, but tomorrow morning, first let's have a meeting, let's get a meeting together with the student body."

So the next day, we did and filled Biddle Hall. There were 680 students up in there. And I was the one, "Have y'all heard what's happening in Greensboro?" And slowly told the story and put it in context and said, "I don't know about y'all but tomorrow morning, I'm gonna wash up and put on my best Sunday go-to-meeting clothes, a little extra sweetwater, and I'm gonna come up to Biddle Hall and I'm gonna walk down Trade to the Square. I'm gonna sit at Woolworth's. So do what you want to or not? This is the time!"

I got up the next morning, washed up, put on a little extra sweetwater and one of my best suits, walked up Biddle Hall and in front of the hall were 228 students saying let's rock and roll. And we walked down to the Square and had organized so that a group would go to Woolworth's, a group would go to Grant's, go to Liggett's, and I was the facilitator and I'm standing on the Square and the group who went to Woolworth's first and said, "Charles, they don't know what to do with us. What should we do?" I said, "Go back and sit. We're gonna continue to do this same thing from Grant."

There was a white guy standing right near me who said, "Young man, what's this all about?" I said, "Who are you?" He said, "I'm a reporter from *The Charlotte Observer*. We heard all about some of the stuff you've been trying to do." The backstory here is that I'd been to a festival 1959 in Vienna, Austria, organized by the Soviet student movement to try to convince us all—students invited from more than 100 different countries—that Soviet communism was a better way of life than democracy. I was invited by a group, Yale, Harvard, white as well as black. I had gotten to know some of those guys. We flew over, had this huge gathering, maybe a thousand different people, and then we were told you can go out and talk about what we were trying to persuade you is a better way of life.

So I went outside, I remember this as clearly as I'm sitting here, I was saying to some of the students of different cultures, "I hear what they're saying, but I believe that democracy is a better way of life. So whatever you're talking about is all good but I'm from the United States of America and we've got a long way to go, but I don't want to walk the walk with the communist and socialist party." And this young man came up to me and said, "No, that ain't right! I'm Paul Robeson Jr. and my daddy who had become such a popular person in the United States, the House Committee on Un-American Activities said he was a communist and he got to a point where he couldn't stay around any longer because they were gonna arrest him and all that, so he went to the Soviet Union." And I said, "Young man, I know your dad. As a matter of fact, I know where you were born, 125th Street in Harlem, and I met your dad, I know him, I was blessed and inspired by him."

One of the things I worked out with the group I was with was that we would get accurate news coverage for the papers back in the United States—*New York Times*, *Washington Post* and all—so there was a report, a story in the *New York Times* the next day saying, "Young Black Male Student Defends Democracy in the Communist Hell Gathering" and they even had a picture and I said, oh crap. And because of that it became enough in the press that I was invited by the House Committee on Un-American Activities to come as a friendly witness before them. And I thought about it and I said, hell yeah, so I went up, I'll never forget this. I was dressed in my finest, went into the room where the meeting was taking place, they hadn't come in yet. I was up there and then the committee came in, the chairman and the others, and set on the podium and the meeting opened and the chairman said, "Mr. Jones, welcome to the House Committee on Un-American Activities. We wanted to just chat with you because we came to appreciate that you were at a festival in Vienna, Austria, and you were defending democracy. Tell us about that." So I said, "Well, first of all, we got a long way to go here in this country. But I believe that democracy is a better way of governance than communism, so I'm going to be working toward evolving with and helping to change the way I'm treated among others." And the chairman was saying, "Well, we wanted to thank you." And I said, "Wait a minute, Mr. Chairman. I appreciate being here as a witness, but what have you done for me lately?" And it was quiet, and then they took a brief recess and came back in and one of the members apologized for the attitude of the chairman and thanked me for having gone to Vienna and having defended democracy and then came down and everyone shook my hand.

On that first march on February 8, 1960, our group went to the different stores, and they didn't know what the heck to do with us, so I told them, "Go sit down." So they ended up closing the lunch counters because they didn't know how to handle us. The black ministers, along with JCSU, helped us organize a boycott of all those lunch counters downtown and other facilities where we could not be served. And the ministers were saying, "Ladies, don't you go down and put your money where you're not respected. You buy clothes but they won't even let you try them on. You all got hats that you had, some new for a couple of years. So you stop spending your money, Belk's, Ivey's and all those places." That started a boycott. I was kind of the leader. As a matter of fact, there's a picture of a picket line right in the middle there, and we were joined by Unitarians. White men and women joined us. The preacher at the Unitarian Church here, Sid Freeman, encouraged his congregation.

So on February 9, the students of my group went down to the City

Council, and Mayor Brookshire was there, and encouraged them to set up a biracial committee to help work out some kind of way to open up these lunch counters because we were gonna be coming back and coming back. They decided to do it and I got a call from the mayor the next day saying, "Jones, we appreciate how you're handling this and we're gonna work to see if we can't get some kind of consensus from the City Council." They set up a meeting, they did bring in six or seven black guys and I got a call from the mayor on July 2 saying, "Mr. Jones, City Council had a meeting last night and Mr. Belk with Belk store said, 'We gotta do something about this boycott. We're losing a lot of money.' And George Ivey Jr. and I, a store down on the next block, said, 'If we don't do something, we're gonna have to file for bankruptcy.'" And he said, "Mr. Jones, there was a discussion and we had a vote and it was to encourage the lunch counter owners who were there, so tomorrow you can go down and you'll be served."

So the next morning, my father J.T. Jones and I went down right on the Square was a drug store and lunch counter, Liggett's, where the Bank of America skyscraper is now, and we walked in—gosh, this gorgeous, tall sister said, "Hi, please come in, we prepared a patch of tables for you. You can see West Trade, East Trade, North Tryon, South Tryon. Please, have a seat." As we walked over, she put her hand up like this and gave a thumbs up. Dad I waited for a minute, then sat at the lunch counter, I think he ordered a hot dog and french fries and I ordered a hamburger and french fries. Some of the worst-tasting coffee in the world but I had a Coke and we sat and slowly ate. And daddy said, "Son, I'm proud of you. The way you handled this, being the leading spokesman, I'm now able—for the first time—to eat and be respected, so thank you, son." And I said, "Well, thank you, dad, but you told me the basic lessons: when to hold 'em, when to fold 'em, when to stand but also when to walk away." And we kind of smiled. At that point, that meal was probably $12, $15 for both of them, and she brought us the check, Daddy paid it, but he also, he also tipped some people, a crisp $5 bill. And he left that as a tip and he and I start walking out and that sister said, "Wait a minute, wait a minute! I can't take this. I've been getting more respect because of how y'all handled this, so put this in your pocket." I looked at Dad, and I knew that was a moment that I had to respect her. It wasn't about tips, it was about her pride and being the sister that served. It was that now I'm getting respect as a waitress from everybody and I'm respected and I conduct myself in a way that I always have, but you're the first black folk that gonna come in and I see myself in what you all are doing. I appreciate the tip, but you're giving me something more valuable than all the money.

* * * * * *

I was arrested about ten times during the Civil Rights Movement. We went down to Montgomery, Alabama, on the Freedom Rides, and joined the students at Friendship College who had been inspired by us here to non-violence. South Carolina wasn't ready, so some of the students made a decision to sit at the lunch counter and get arrested and rather than posting bail, to spend thirty days on the York County chain gang. A good friend of mine, Charles Sherrod, contacted me and said, "Charles did you hear about what happened at Friendship?" I said yeah. He said, "I'm inspired by what they did, because that's kind of what we do. Let's go down and join them, sit at the lunch counter, get arrested and spend thirty days on the York County chain gang. Hard labor." I said, "Are you serious?" He said, "Yeah." So we went down to Rock Hill to Friendship College. The guys who had been, they got arrested, were sentenced to thirty days of hard labor on the chain gang. Sherrod and I came in about four days later, went to the same lunch counter. A man named Cecil

Ivory, a brother, met us there. He had also joined the students but he chose not to go to jail because he was a leader there in Rock Hill. So we went down, let him know, we went down and sat at the same lunch counter, got arrested, were sentenced to thirty days of hard labor, [singing] "Uh! That's the sound of the men, uh, workin' on the chain, uh, gang."

We joined, Sherrod and I, Diane Nash and Ruby Doris Smith, two young ladies who were active in the movement too. They came but they wouldn't put them on the chain gang. So Sherrod and I went and got to the York County chain gang, went in and let the young people from Friendship know. There were two pretty good-sized cells with bunk beds, three or two, black on one side, a hallway about 12 feet, white on the other side, and [laughs] Sherrod and I started having a little service in the mornings when we'd wake up, we'd sing songs. We both were still students at that point, selective scripture and we'd started saying, and the jury saying, "Shut up that damn fuss."

"Ain't gonna let nobody know turn me around."

"I said, Shut up that damn fuss, boy!"

"We gonna keep on a'walkin', uh, keep on ..."

"Put 'em in the hole, put 'em in solitary confinement."

"Walkin' up to freedom."

No blankets and we were, I'll never forget this, about two o'clock in the morning, and Sherrod, still awake said, "Charles, what we gonna do about this society we live in? We can't continue to encourage it, to treat us like they have." I said, "We're gonna build the Lord's community where all of God's children, both the black folk and white live together in harmony."

* * * * * *

Years, later, in the '80s, I was blessed to have helped organize Biddleville as the chairman of the Biddleville Community Organization. We met down at Smallwood Presbyterian Church. Among other things, we had to organize the Biddleville Smallwood Community Organization where we brought both communities together. By then, the law allowed black folks to buy wherever they could and wanted to. There was a white realtor, a young guy, who would say to the people who lived in Smallwood, "Whoa, they're comin'! Whoa, they're comin'! But we got some place you can go and we'll buy your house and help you move, get you another place." They were selling the houses $20,000 to $30,000 less than their value and so we helped people understand that they could buy those houses and they did, and the neighborhood then integrated. Mostly white folks left, however—most all of them did.

So now as things have evolved in the last ten to fifteen years, this neighborhood has become one of the most developed neighborhoods in Charlotte. It has houses that are $400,000, $500,000 or more; black and white folk have moved in and become very much involved in the community organization. So there came a moment, and my grandma used to say, "Boy, don't just hang around when you've done all you can. Move on." So I got newer officers and president of the community organization and now the meeting is every third Thursday. Smallwood Presbyterian Church is full—white, black, everybody. So I have moved on.

Yesterday, I was watching a movie, a documentary: "Freedom Riders." All of a sudden it came as I was watching it; I was one of the Freedom Riders. There were a couple of moments when we were coming into Montgomery and they picked you up in the middle where the police had guns pointed. They were told to hold their guns up, not at us, and they showed a picture of that. When I saw the whole history of the Freedom Riders, sitting there watching that screen, and then seeing my own face. I said, "Oh, my God.

Thank you, Jesus."

Today, we're living in strange times and I'm so proud of our young activists. You had a sense that these protests were coming, but you didn't quite understand what was going to be the behavior, particularly of the young black men. There was a moment or two, if you remember, most everybody else was very well behaved, protesting with dignity, a small number of people doing the violence. But that number is getting smaller, so I know we have evolved to another place. These young people are carrying on the work we did with dignity and effectiveness too. The brothers and sisters are walking with pride. And they are listening. I'm so proud, man. And I'm proud to be an inspiration.

COLIN PINKNEY

Colin Pinkney is one of Charlotte's most inspirational leaders. He has forged deep connections in the community not only by sharing his personal story of emotional pain and poverty, but by offering our youth a powerful blueprint for change, hope, and progress. In 2008, he founded the groundbreaking "We Are World Class" book club for male high school students, helping legions of urban teens graduate from high school on time. His transparent, no-holds-barred approach to problem solving, coupled with his intuitive ability to forge an array of grassroots partnerships, has garnered distinguished recognition from former Mayor of Charlotte Anthony Foxx, former Governor of North Carolina Beverly Perdue, and NBA legend and Charlotte Hornets' CEO Michael Jordan. Since 2013, Pinkney has served as Executive Director of The Harvest Center of Charlotte, a faith-based organization focused on helping the homeless, poor, and unemployed in our city.

TEN MEN

My brother's name is Bill. We just buried him. He is probably the most intelligent man I've ever known. He's probably the most talented, gifted man I've ever known, the most articulate man I've ever known. And yet he's probably the most troubled and conflicted man I've ever known.

I never really appreciated that until the night he died. He was fifty-seven. Like a lot of people who see other people keep doing bad things, I had kind of a judgment that he had better control of that than he was displaying, that he could get a handle on it. That there was a tipping point where it was no longer about things he couldn't control, but it was about his intentionality to be that way. I took a very external view of his behavior. And I didn't see the conflict as much as I saw just the controversy it always caused.

Just to be so talented, to be so gifted. I used to look at his paintings and be mesmerized. I was his biggest fan. I would look at his artwork and was like wow, man. There was stuff I'd look at and it would make you laugh uncontrollably. It would make you cry just making you see how powerful it was. I never saw it through his eyes until he died. And when he died I realized the painting was his therapy, that he was painting to heal. I look at his artwork totally different now. He was trying to fix broken stuff in our life, in our family.

He'd painted a picture of a mother sitting at the base of a tree. The tree is filled with real kids hanging over the branches and the mother's down there reading to the kids. That was never my family's reality. We never lived like that. But most of Bill's paintings, he was trying to depict something real.

If you look at some of his work, he called himself a contemporary jazz artist. He did a lot of music, trumpeters and saxophonists and nightclub singers, and a lot of people don't know it still, that he would paint and intentionally put somewhere on one of the instruments, "Pinkney." Not as his signature on the painting. The piano wasn't a Baldwin, it was a Pinkney.

The cello was a Pinkney. The music was coming from our family. He was doing his own therapy. We've only got one of his paintings in our house, it's a print, and the day he died I let myself slow down enough to think about, whoa, what just happened?

I was on the phone. My brother, my sister, his daughter, and my brother-in-law were in Kannapolis in the hospital, and we were on the phone for an hour waiting for a nurse to show up to tell us what's going on, because we're trying to find him. My mother's looking for him, but nobody else is looking for Bill because everyone knows Bill's being Bill—he gets aloof sometimes. He's doin' what he does. Mamma said, "No, you need to find Bill." Finally, she called the police.

We're waiting on the phone and the police officer walks out. I'm on the phone with my wife and the lady says, "I think we found your loved one. William Alton Pinkney is deceased."

I had to let that sink in.

I went back to our childhood where I always personalize our family trauma, to me and my issue and what it caused in my life. Then the thing that dawned on me was that my mother made him man of the house at fourteen. I realized then that what we saw as something courageous and something noble—because if anybody could do it, Bill could do it—what was revealed to me in that moment was what we thought was a celebration was really his burden. And he didn't get to celebrate that. We did. Just like his paintings, we look at his artwork and we go, "Wow! Oh my God, now I see it."

I can't remember the last time my brother Bill went to the church, but we would have family calls every Saturday morning. The Saturday before he passed, which would have been January the 7th, we had a family call. It was 7:00 in the morning on a Saturday, and we were gonna pray and then talk about Mama's birthday party.

TEN MEN

A year and a half prior, I had told Bill and my mother and my siblings—again, because I'm in this work now and I understand mental illness and co-dependency and all the areas that people act out in that aren't healthy and are destructive—I told my family, "I made a decision for me and my family. I'm not gonna have anything to do with Bill or Mama until they fix their relationship and stop living this co-dependent way." I had never talked to my brother since.

The Saturday before he died, he beeped in on the conference call and he listened. He usually gets in; he's very boisterous: "What y'all talkin' about now?" "Don't be talkin' about me!" "Look, I'm tired of y'all!" and he would go off and everybody would back up. I had taken the stance a year ago that I had had enough and backed off. The last time I heard his voice was on that phone call the Saturday before he died. My sister said, "Colin, why don't you close this out in prayer?" and I prayed for every one of my siblings by name. Started from oldest to the youngest. And I called Bill's name and I said, "Lord, thank you for my brother, thank you for his gift to this family, all that he is." I said nothing negative—I don't pray negative stuff. Less than thirty-six hours later, he passed.

* * * * * *

My dad left when I was nine years old, and when he left, my mother dubbed my fourteen-year-old brother, Bill, the man of the house. There were seven kids in that house. My daddy, we knew he was still around; he was at Fort Bragg for a while and then he disappeared, went away. Fayetteville was my hometown. After my father left, it was like the floodgates opened up. I saw every manner of perversion, of abuse, of drug, of alcohol. I saw stuff that nine-year-old boys ain't got no business seeing. And here's the thing—my whole context as I was growing up was I was the only one going through that. I didn't even contextualize that my sisters and brothers were all going through the same thing. It was just me; I was all, "Woe is me. Why don't I have a dad? Where's my daddy?"

When my daddy split, he split. I grew up when there was no power in the house for weeks at a time and we would burn candles for lights. Our friends didn't even know what we were living through. We lived in kind of a middle-suburban neighborhood. The only thing he did for us is get us that house because the military made him get us a house. They wouldn't let us live on a military base. If you get divorced in the military, the non-military spouse has to leave the base. That was the rule. So my daddy still lived on the base and we knew he lived in Fort Bragg. We couldn't go to Fort Bragg. We saw all this destruction, this chaos, this madness, all five of my sisters pregnant before they left high school, all of them. My brother Bill at a young age started playing with marijuana, that went to crack, that went to heroin, that went to all kind of lifelong drug abuse.

* * * * * *

The book club has become something very structured, but initially it was just a grassroots-level attempt by a principal at a high-needs school to get a handle on what is going on with young black men, particularly, specifically. At the school level, leadership is everything. It isn't enough to just look the part. There's some groups out here, and I like them, they're doing some stuff, they're trying to put an African-American male in the classroom, in leadership, so young black men growing up can see that growing up through school. That doesn't matter if there's no leadership.

I started this book club a few years ago years ago at Olympic High School after a young girl was killed by her boyfriend. She was a cheerleader, and her friends were trying to tell her you need to leave that dude alone, he ain't nothing but trouble. He told her, "I promise you, if you ever try to leave me I'm going to kill you." She tried to leave, he kept his promise. So the school's in an uproar; they start having all these issues, acting out. This is right about the time right before WorldStarHipHop when these kids would get on YouTube and videotape some of the most crazy stuff you'd ever think. I had just spoken at West Charlotte, a lady with Communities in Schools said, "Mr. Pinkney, come do that talk over here with the boys at Olympic, because we got trouble." They put four hundred boys in the auditorium, all black, and they said, "Just tell them the truth. These boys aren't listening to nobody; they're acting out in school." So I went and told the truth, I told them my story growing up at home without a father.

I told them the about my big brother who played pro football for six years. He had six sons, all born out of wedlock except one, by three different women. Now the only noble thing that he did was he made sure he stayed around in their life, he took care of them, they had the money they needed, they all went to college and graduated. My nephew signed the biggest contract in the history of the NFL for a non-quarterback six years ago, $66 million. He won't even speak to his dad because my brother never married his mother and they had three boys together. I'm talking about the floodgates opening up. I'm talking about generational, systemic destructive decay. My brother never married his mother, but they had three sons together. All them boys had college degrees. So that's what I told the book club. I just told them my story and I told them, "I know where you're at. I know what you're going through. Y'all think y'all got it bad. Listen to me, trust me when I tell you, I know. I know what you're doing. I know what the struggle is. I know it's real. But you don't have to live that way."

About two weeks later I got a call from the school. They said, "Mr. Pinkney, these boys want to talk to you again. Can you come back over here?" So I started asking myself how do we make sure this makes a difference? We gotta make sure these boys graduate, that's the big deal, so we said let's start with that. Now I can't really influence graduation rate per se, but what can I influence? I ain't trying to teach algebra and math and I ain't trying to be a teacher, but we can read. I got books everywhere. So I said, "Why don't we just read some books?" First, I'm reading the books. Before you know it, we're buying books and everybody's reading them. Before you know it, the boys are asking, "Mr. Pinkney, what's our next book?" Before you know it, the first few years, boys thought they were being penalized when they were being put in book club; they actually thought that. One of my guys just graduated from Hampton University; he's now about to become an Air Force officer. When he came into book club, he said, "The only other person who made me read was my mama and I only did it because she's my mama. But Mr. Pinkney, he make it fun."

As adults we tend to totally underestimate what our boys can handle and are willing to read. We are part of the problem. We're pigeonholing them to stay in their lane. The most academic book we read was Cornel West's and Tavis Smiley's *The Rich and the Rest of Us: A Poverty Manifesto*. We read a true story about a black man sharecropper who didn't learn how to read until he was ninety-eight years old. We read Hill Harper's book *Letters to a Young Brother*. We read *The Pact: Three Young Men Make a Promise and Fulfill a Dream* to become doctors. They were Johns Hopkins guys. Street thugs, then they realized they're getting in trouble too much. The pact was, let's all go to college and become doctors and they did it. But the book's about the reality that their success wasn't a straight line neither. They still had some bumps and bruises.

TEN MEN

Soon we started attracting boys of all races; you can't just have an all-black boys book club at a public school. So we had some Caucasians, some Asians, Indian, Arab boys in the book club. I got ninety-something Facebook friends from book club. *Life is so Good*. We had a couple of Latino boys in there, I asked them, "What would you like to read?" One boy said, "There's a book called *Buried Onions*, it's just like *The Pact*, we should read that." It's about these little Latino boys. True story, that grew up in Compton, and were in a gang. So then you have black boys looking through the lens of Latino boys. I got people always pushing me, "You gotta read this book," but what I found out is if it ain't true, if it ain't something where they say, "I know a guy like that," then they aren't interested. They don't even want to read historical literature, Shakespeare. We were looking at Michelle Alexander's *The New Jim Crow*, we need to get a book for this spring.

* * * * * *

The book club has four rules: Read, Respect, Reciprocate, and Represent. Read means we will read; there's nothing we can't talk about but we got to read about it first. We can talk about what's going wrong with your family, we can talk about your girlfriend issues, we can talk about your court issues. I have one boy in court right now. We gotta read about it first. We gotta have context. That lays a foundation. Now that we've read, let's talk about it. We say, read, respect. Respect means we're gonna talk. If I talk, you're listening. If you're talking, I'm listening. I'm not gonna talk over you. I can't call you names, I can't degrade you, I can't call you out, I can't use even funny nigger words because you all think it's cool. Read, respect, and then reciprocate. We got this powerful way of reciprocating. Reciprocate means positive affirmation for whatever you do that's good. Represent means that we will commit that everyone in this book club graduates on time because we always have some boys who are at risk. Today, we've had 100 percent graduation rate.

The book club lets me extend myself that to those boys. And I know those boys see me in that role. When I go to the school, those boys light up and it blows my mind. They know I'm honest with them; I'm gonna tell them the truth. I told those boys, "I'm gonna tell you something that nobody knows right now." We read my brother's story. I told them about my brother's art, how he painted that portrait of the architect who designed Duke University. Here's the crazy part, Phil Freelon, who designed the Harvey Gantt Museum here, and the chief architect of the new Smithsonian Museum, he and my brother went to N.C. State together. He was a year behind Bill. When I went to Duke University after Bill's death to represent our family, I was talking to Phil and I showed him the obituary. He said, "Bill Pinkney's your brother?"

JUSTIN HARLOW

The face of Charlotte's Historic West End is changing fast as young profession-als—white and black, old and young alike—migrate to the area to enjoy its stately architecture and close proximity to Uptown. Among the area's most dynamic, vis-ible new leaders is Justin Harlow, a young dentist from Atlanta, who along with his attorney wife Kiara, purchased a home in the historic Biddleville community in 2014. A graduate of Emory University and the University of North Caro-lina at Chapel Hill's School of Dentistry, as well as a member of Alpha Phi Alpha fraternity, Harlow has been a tireless force in reinvigorating Biddleville, serv-ing as president of the neighborhood's association and steeping himself in the area through volunteerism, mentoring, and community advocacy.

TEN MEN

I don't have a story of growing up in desperate poverty. We definitely weren't rich, but we weren't poor either. I would call us a lower-middle-class, two-parent household. My dad has a degree in business; both my parents were first-generation college students. They went to a historically black college, Albany State University in Albany, Georgia. My dad is originally from New York, had a basketball scholarship to Albany State, and went on to own a small business, chauffeuring, transportation business. My dad was hit hard by the recession so now, as he nears retirement, he does some business administration things with Fulton County government. My mother has been in corporate America for a long time. She worked for UPS for a while, worked for Delta for a while, big Atlanta companies and middle-management type of things. She, too, is reaching retirement and has tapered off, in the insurance field. I have an older sister in Atlanta who's an assistant district attorney in Fulton County. My brother's a corporate finance analyst for Hewlett-Packard in Houston. If you're looking at a map, I grew up on the south side of Atlanta, between the airport and Cascade. I went to Atlanta Public Schools, then Emory University and University of North Carolina-Chapel Hill for dental school and graduate school. I'm a member of a fraternity, Alpha Phi Alpha, and my association with that has helped my professional development and valuing networks and valuing black networks specifically. I'm in a group practice now in the university area, in University Executive Park. I've been practicing for almost three years, the same amount of time we've been in this house, here in Five Points.

Growing up in Atlanta, I saw it change vastly, especially pre-Olympics and post-Olympics in the '90s and it turning essentially into this black-ish mecca. Some of that is because of the entertainment industry is down there, but it's been a growing city and an affordable region as well. Charlotte is playing catch-up to that now. It's not trying to be Atlanta and it never will be, which I think is a good thing, but what drives my civic activism and interest is that I've always been a part of networks that help cities thrive. My community involvement is really a paying-it-forward type of thing. I had so many mentors growing up that helped me, guided me in various ways, so I just want to do the same. I've been very blessed to be where I am—as a homeowner, as a husband and father, and professionally as a dentist, still under the age of thirty.

Charlotte was not my choice; it was my wife's choice, really. She's from Elgin, South Carolina, about forty minutes northeast of Columbia, and she has some family here in Charlotte. It was more of that Charlotte's a great place; it's not Atlanta, but it's not Columbia either, a great middle ground with a great job market. She sold me on it. When I came to Chapel Hill for dental school, I had classmates from Charlotte, so I would come with them to CIAA weekend and that was my first experience of Charlotte. I came for the Democratic National Convention. I've always had a political interest anyway, and of course a black president being nominated, that played its own role in it too. That helped me see that Charlotte, this is a different place. I almost equate how the Olympics put Atlanta on this global scale and maybe the DNC helped create a little bit of that for Charlotte. CIAA, I equate to AUC homecomings down in Atlanta for Morehouse and Spelman because we used to party there all the time when I was at Emory. Add that to the fact that it's easier coming from a North Carolina dental school to get a North Carolina dental license than to go back to Georgia. I was all about, she's out of law school, I'm out of dental school, we had no kids, we're young, twenty-five at the time, so it was like, let's just live Uptown, let's rent a condo and we can hang out all the time. We didn't know much about Charlotte, where to live. Our plan was to just rent. But at the same time, we wanted to be fiscally prudent and we knew that if this was going to be our permanent place, rent over time becomes a sunken cost. There's no value in it.

You hear about Ballantyne, you hear Huntersville, but we weren't trying to be suburban like that. My wife's all into interior design and architecture stuff, and she saw these new Craftsman-style bungalow homes close to downtown. You have a couple pockets in Charlotte that have that same set-up—Plaza Midwood, NoDa, Dilworth—but the difference, those are more known places, so the value of those homes were significantly higher, because those are branded areas. You look online and what the heck is Biddleville and what the heck is Smallwood, and you look west of Uptown and we'd always heard "don't live west, don't live east." But we drove over here and we found the agent who was listing all of these different new homes over here, and he toured us around and showed us some of the things that they were selling and building. He ended up showing us this one, which was eighty percent built at the time, and we just fell in love with it.

Part of what sells this neighborhood is that we're so close to Uptown. If you went upstairs to my bedroom, you can see Duke Energy and Bank of America Corporate Center from my window. Still, it's not considered part of Uptown. This is a larger-scale issue, how cities have disenfranchised certain areas. It's interesting how interstates were built in this city particularly. If you look at where 277 does a loop around the city, and I-77 goes perpendicular to it, we're just west of there. You have to cross a bridge, literally that idea of crossing the train tracks, crossing the bridge. So they don't see us as part of Uptown and I would say that we see ourselves as an extension of Uptown but we're not Uptown. The media, if a crime happened right here on this corner, they wouldn't say, 1.1 miles from Trade and Tryon—because that's what we are, right here—they wouldn't say 1.1 miles from Uptown; they would say West Charlotte. There's a larger play there, some of that we can't control because it's rooted in people's minds. I cross that bridge, I'm in

West Charlotte, no matter how vast West Charlotte might be.

If you look at the census block from here, it literally is the interstate to the Brookshire, not Uptown. Our median income of our census block is like $23,000. The crime stats are higher because it includes some stuff going farther down Rozzelles Ferry where it gets more industrial. Our biggest challenge is, we got to get more private investment over here because some people, they don't care what your home looks like, people will drive over here and say, these houses look nice, but we don't have a retail corridor, we don't have a commercial corridor. Our commercial corridor is Uptown, and that would be OK if Uptown included us in all of their data, but there's a gap there. I think the streetcar might help with that when it gets built because now you have some connectivity measures and we see how permanent modes of transportation help spur development.

One of my goals has been to literally change the narrative of what neighborhoods can be on Charlotte's West Side. Even the small stuff—getting a logo, getting a website, helping attract people to the area because you can have a digital footprint now so people know what the heck Biddleville is. Because when you say SouthPark, when you say Plaza Midwood, you know what that is. When you say South End, you know what that is. When you say Biddleville, it may be like, where's that? I'll tell some folks, it's right by Johnson C. Smith, and they still might say, where's that? Huh? That university's been around here 150 years. That's sad.

Dr. Carter has done a good job in trying to articulate the vision on what he wants the surrounding area of Johnson C. Smith to be. He describes it as this Georgetown type of college, George Washington University type of feel. You can have coffee shops because this university is tucked in a neighborhood. Emory in the Druid Hills area of Atlanta is tucked in a neighborhood, and we've got little pizza shops and boutiques and dessert shops and stuff, like Franklin Street in Chapel Hill. West Trade and Beatties Ford Road could be that. Right now, the students have to go Uptown to do anything. There's nothing around the university outside of whatever's going on at the cafe outside of Mosaic Village and that's not really picking up the way it could have. And they don't come to this brewery. If I was in college I would be all over this thing, but they don't do that. There's no sit-down places around here, traditional restaurants or anything like that.

We've had some conversation with retail folks, grocery stores, and coffee shop places and they'll always tell you, based on the demographic research they do, this area doesn't generate enough income. The household incomes aren't high enough yet to make sense for them to come in. Trader Joe's, Starbucks, Panera. This is definitely not your Starbucks-Panera type of area. But there's a parking shop lot that's been empty from what I understand fifteen, twenty years and it's a prime location for a small-scale grocery store. Even the smaller concept stores like Aldi and Walmart Neighborhood Market where it's not a huge big box, but you still have these smaller concept entities that some of these stores are trying to do now. Al Austin has worked very hard for this community and tried to recruit something like that.

Everyone has to play a role in changing the narrative over. That's the only way businesses are going to come over here. If not, they will feel like, if the people that live here don't spend their money here, then why am I gonna spend my money here? I get my hair cut at No Grease because I want them to be successful, and I go to the cafe and I'll have a drink because I want them to do well. If I ever build a dental office over here I'm gonna go to Darrel and say be my architect, draw my dental office. I'm trying to support the businesses over here and hope that comes back tenfold to me.

There's tons of potential here. You've got folks who are buying second lots and properties who are wanting to stay and take advantage of the economic advantages of this area. Everywhere around the city center things are popping up—Villa Heights, NoDa, Belmont. So the only way to go is west, because this is the last frontier. We just have to make it attractive enough and be patient. This isn't an overnight thing, that's for sure. But we have to have enough people pushing the issue. I think this area has suffered so long with no one advocating for it.

I want this area to recognize its potential and make it a safer place to live, continue to recruit and have different types of faces moving in but also branding itself as this is just as good of a place to live as South End or Plaza Midwood. If we can get a logo, get some street sign toppers so when people drive down Rozzelles Ferry, they see signs on every intersection corner Biddleville/ Smallville. I think we do a poor job of branding everything as West End.

This particular area we're slowly trying to rebrand is Five Points, which used to be a five-way intersection; now it's a four-way intersection. The neighborhood is changing dramatically, it's much more integrated along race and generational lines. Most of the white people moving in here are early-thirties, they have kids and so I am slightly younger than them but we're all in the same kind of generation. Now, let's be clear, I'm not race blind, we don't live in a post-racial America. I try to be as activist-friendly as I can without being militant. I'm certainly not a militant guy, but I would say that does help because I can speak to having a family with them. Talking about schools, I have skin in the game now, with a child. We can have conversations around real estate investment with them. I can have professional conversations with them and I think that's a difference that some of the older residents can't have either because they have resentment there because the neighborhood's changing or because there's just a true generational disconnect.

I'm trying to be that bridge. I'm black and I'm always going to be black, so I'm going to be able to talk to black neighbors in a very different level than these white neighbors are going to be able to talk to black neighbors. They might never say it out loud, but the white folks will see me differently because I'm a dentist or because I wear loafers and a collared shirt and I'm purposely and intentionally trying to understand the dynamic around my image in their eyes and how that plays a role in them accepting me. It shouldn't be that way and I'm still going to be me. There's a wavelength there, maybe because I have a white education as well, so there's all of those components. There's still that balancing act to play. Some of that's politics and real life. Who knows if we'll live in this area forever or not? But if I can say I helped get that or I helped create something like that here, then that's a step forward.

I just want this community to be able to grow together to prove that cities can have communities that aren't homogenous communities and helping it advocate for themselves a little more. Just small neighborhood things, more neighborhood social events, bringing people together, inviting people into your home. The older black people will say to me about older white folks, "Well, they don't ever speak when they're walking by." It's because so many of these transplants we have coming to Charlotte are from the North, so it's more a Northern mentality than it is a white mentality. Some of these black folks have been here fifty years; these are Southern grown black people. When you're older, you're looking for that deference, like I'm not speaking to you until you're speaking to me. That exists in black culture, but I don't know if that exists in white culture.

My goal, by being able to relate a little more, or maybe from a socioeconomic level to these white people, is look, you gotta speak to these folks. Unfortunately, it may feel like sucking up, but that's just what it is. You moved here; they were here before you. You'll find that a lot of these folks are very religious driven, they all go to the same church, they're very Presbyterian-style folks, they're all very mission based in their faith. I'm not the most religious person, and I would say that's my generation also, we are slowly leaving the big black churches and becoming more spiritual and faith-based rather than religion-based. These white folks moving in, they're open to that, they just didn't know. It's easier, because if a black lady sitting on their porch and she's seventy-five years old and she's sitting there, they don't want to feel like they're being awkward by approaching their home, like they're trespassing or taking liberties. So there's this eggshell moment that you're walking on. I'm trying to find my niche and be that bridge and say, "Look, it's OK for you to do that. You're going to build some social capital if you do it." Otherwise, we get these neighborhoods within a neighborhood.

We're living within the same place but we're not living together. One of my top priorities is community advocacy, just trying to create a more open social environment. Before you apply for Neighborhood Matching Grants, let's just learn who we are together. Let's do movie night, let's have a community dinner, let's have a neighborhood picnic, let's do a neighborhood cleanup. We do all those things. Some of those things I helped create; some of those things were here before and I just helped build on them. One of the things I really helped build is one of these larger Five Points communities—Wesley Heights, Seversville, and Biddleville—because all these neighborhoods are going through a similar style transition. We've done some food truck events up there, get people out of their homes, see who else is in this community, walk your dog up there and bring your granddaughter, the old folks, and you bring your dog and your stroller. Let's be together.

We don't have to be Cherry or we don't have to be other parts of the city where it used to be very black and now there ain't no blacks. We can be different. We can have both things. You can have gay and straight people living next to each other. You can have faith-based people and non-faith-based people next to each other, black, white, rich, poor, whatever, and all live in the same community. A lot of these older folks, when I say advocacy, their biggest thing fifteen years ago was prostitutes over here and it was crime-ridden. So they got rid of a lot of the crime and they've advocated for pushing prostitution out of this neighborhood at least. They say, "We've done enough, we like our community, we don't want it to change any more." And our thing is, let's go an extra step. Now you've gotten that out of the way, let's work on better lighting, let's work on grounding these power lines. Let's work on adding stop signs and speed limit signs to make it a better neighborhood from a public safety standpoint. Or let's go a step further— let's make sure this school gets better because now we have a failing school right over here at Bruns Academy in a non-failing neighborhood. Let's move the needle more. Keep pushing that. Don't settle.

Also, let's not just look inward to our community but outward. Let's work with other parts of the community, the YMCA, the Boys & Girls Club. Let's help tutor over here at Bruns Academy. Let's get in touch with our local M&F black bank. We've got folks in this neighborhood, professionals like me. I'd love to put a dental office over here one day. We've got a personal trainer who'd love to put a CrossFit gym over here, it's down the road, but now that you've put in some of these infrastructure things, you've helped the economy of the area with your home values, so now let's take it a step further and drive some business into this area. Because if we just live here but still work everywhere else, you want this eat/work/play/educate environment. That's really what an urban neighborhood is supposed to be.

DAMIAN JOHNSON

Damian Johnson is one of Charlotte's most admired entrepreneurs. Since graduating from Johnson C. Smith University in 1997, Damian, along with his twin brother Jermaine and business partner Charlie Petty, has built No Grease Inc., a barbering chain and school, into one of Charlotte's most recognizable and respected brands. From its clean, comfortable environs to its spiffy bow-tied barbers, No Grease embodies its "It's Not What We Do. It's How We Do It." mantra. Damian's impassioned message of economic empowerment and community pride has meanwhile served as a catalyst behind No Grease's talented workforce—mostly African-American men from a wide variety of socioeconomic backgrounds—in North Carolina and Georgia.

TEN MEN

When the riots broke out in Uptown, we were getting all these phone calls from people who were watching it on CNN and saying, "They're right in front of y'all's shop." When we went down there the next morning, we see all the broken glass and all these broken windows next door to our shop, and there's nothing damaged at ours. It was amazing nobody vandalized us. It was emotional; it was humbling.

We were spared, I believe, because of the relationships we've built with our community during our twenty years in business. The free haircuts, the advice we've given to the young men who have been coming to our shops for years, the simple recognition of saying, "What's up?" to a cat when they walk past the shop in that community, the students we've taught and the jobs we've created. Those guys know us. They may have left us alone, thinking, "Yo, that's No Grease."

A twenty-five-year-old that's down there in the riot was five years old when we opened our first shop. If he grew up here in Charlotte, he is familiar with No Grease and knows it's a black business. Our customers have always felt a sense of ownership of our shops, they feel like it is theirs, too— and it really is. Many of the people protesting could relate to us as a business that has survived and thrived in spite of the black-on-black crime, despite the police brutality, despite the economic challenges we're having—we've survived in spite of. It's a special relationship.

There's something unique about the dynamics of a barber-client. When someone sits down, they could be the cockiest man alive or even a billionaire, but there's a humbling position that they assume when they sit in that chair and let you go to work. There's a certain level of trust and confidence they must have in their barber to let them operate. The person in the chair lets their guard down. One thing I tell barbers is that a client more than likely has been getting his hair cut longer than you've been cutting. Because if you're a thirty-year-old barber and you've only been cutting ten years and a fifteen-year-old boy gets in your chair, he's been getting his hair cut for probably fourteen years so he knows certain things about how a barber should feel. It's something he knows, that he senses, because he's been getting his hair cut since he was a baby. They have to trust their barber, and they want to.

After touching so many people all these years, there's something in the human touch, a rawness and human nature of the physical human contact, that creates a special bridge. And then you talk about male-on-male contact, they're going to know, that didn't feel right, because men don't let men touch them. So it's going to be a heightened sensitivity about whether you're confident or not or are genuine or not. From a man-on-man contact, it's very heightened when dealing with each other. I think that's some of the untold stories of how the barber and the client connect. And usually once those two connect, those are bonds that last forever. It's beyond the barber chair, beyond that whole experience. It's because of that humility that a man has to take to get in your chair, to trust you to touch him. You're touchin' his face and stuff; you know, men don't do that. I think all those dynamics make you start dealing with boys or men in a whole different way. From my experience, we learned how to take that outside of the barbershop, outside of the actual barber chair. We use those same gifts and take it outside of the shop to establish trust.

* * * * * *

The barbering school helps us identify and develop employees who could be successful working at No Grease. I can get a good feel for who I'm dealing with. If he's on drugs, we can get him clean before he finishes school. Whatever you're battling, if you got some issues with your family, we deal with that first here before we get you on the professional side making money, because if you start making money, it's just going to make that twice as challenging. There's no way around it, dealing primarily with black men. You're going to have to deal with the personal issues. You're gonna have to become the social worker, the uncle, father, the big brother. You're gonna have to become all those things, just to get the production that you're looking for. If you're not willing to take that on, there's no way we'll be in business. I remember thinking, you just throw them all away, until you get that perfect one. That doesn't work. You might get one cat that comes in focused and ready for everything one out of every ten years.

In our school, we get people anywhere from eighteen to fifty. Many of them have very stained backgrounds, from drug dealers to murderers, to guys who've compromised a lot of things in their life to get to that place and say, "I gotta do better with my life." Most of them have tried everything and they're like, "Yo, I've always wanted to cut hair but I just never could." We get them all. People who've done corporate America for years and say they just didn't see it as a profession.

Most don't realize this, but historically barbering was the catalyst for black wealth. Post-slavery, the late 1800s, early 1900s, it was the wealth generator for blacks. Blacks were literally buying their freedom with barbering. Those barbers weren't cutting black clients. Their clients were white clients. In many cases, they got set up by their masters right after slavery. Their masters made deals to do business with them because, first, they were making their hair look good, but also they knew they could turn over a dollar. It was, "I'll set up the shop for you; you pay me a lease." That's pretty much what went on from the late 1800s up into the '50s and '60s. There's a moment in American history for at least fifty years or so that black barbers were the predominant service providers for all haircuts in the country. Think about the type of wealth they were generating at that time because we didn't have any money to get our haircuts. They're cutting white folks. I remember meeting an older white man years ago and he would say, "I never let anybody but a black person cut my hair."

It's a very segregated industry. I'm not that old but literally when I started cutting hair, either it was a black shop or a white shop. You know black people don't go into white shops anyway, but white people weren't coming unless they were older white men who had gotten their hair cut by a black man most of their lives. There was a group of white men who were familiar coming into white shops, but that was rare. So there's been a sea change to what we see today. This white boy comes in the barbershop with his father. I said, "You got a picture in your mind of what the hair's gonna look like?" And he pulls out a picture and shows me a picture of Odell Beckham. He's blond but ain't no mistaking; he's black with curly hair. This boy is a white boy with straight hair. His hair ain't gonna do that. Oh, the game has changed. His daddy's like, "Can you come close to it?" In all my years, that was unheard of to have a white kid, first of all come to a black barber, show me a picture of a black man and say, "I want my hair cut like that." When I saw that, I said, "The game is over." It's no longer what it was. They don't see color like we see it. I'm not saying he didn't see this black man, but he was beyond it. He was like, "I wanna be like this man right here." He couldn't have been more than twelve.

* * * * * *

I remember when my mother put the clippers in our hand to cut each other's hair, like "I can't afford to keep taking you out for a haircut." And my mom was a stylist. When you talk about family, the female is usually the leader. Especially when you think about it, I'm a '70s baby, grew up in the '80s, became a man in the '90s. That's how I look at it. So most of us, we're probably that last generation that had a dad in the household as a collective, as a group. By the time you get to the '90s, there's a lot of single parenting going on. We had these strong mothers that were just replacing the black man in the '70s. The '70s was that time when these mothers just had to step up and be everything. That's what my mom was. The way my mom raised me, she was tougher than a lot of men. Just the way she carried herself, the way the discipline was in the house, so when she told us to pick up the clippers, it was almost like your father telling you, "I ain't got no money to get your hair cut."

We became good at cutting our own hair, and soon kids from the neighborhood would come down into our basement. If you know anything about a Buffalo basement, it ain't no finished basement—it was cold walls, cold everything. We put some light on, put a chair in, maybe a little bit of music, and created this atmosphere where young men could come and just talk as we cut hair. When I think about No Grease, we just multiplied that. We honed it a little better, gave it some bells and whistles, but it's the same thing. They feel comfortable exchanging, they're not being judged, they may be being guided, mentored; they can be expressive or just receive.

I was born in the '70s, grew up in the '80s, so we came from looking at hustlers and seeing how they move and operate and how so many people were attracted to those surface things. So we understood how to maneuver in that way because when you deal with black men, if you're not producing, you're gonna lose their interest. They're gone. Some of it can seem superficial or surface stuff but it's necessary when you have so many distractions for young men, black men especially. You're gonna have something in front of them to keep them focused.

I used to feel funny when people came in and said, "Y'all so clean. Y'all so neat. You guys look so professional." I was like, "Should we look any other way?" They were saying this before we were even doing the bowties. We used to all have smocks on, but now, it don't even matter. Black, white, anybody who comes into our shop—we get the same thing. I came from the Timberland boots and baggy pants. That's how we used to dress as barbers; we used to put a smock on. I know what they're saying, it's like, "Yo, I can bring my child to this." My little white son, my black son, because as a parent, I don't care if you hood, I don't care if you straight hood, but if you see a young black man dressed like that cutting hair, that's an impression that you're putting on that young man who's getting his hair cut. You can't beat that impression for a kid. That there's an option—I don't have to sag my pants and get respect. These guys look cool. Listen to the music they listen to; look how the people are swarming to them. This is an option for me. I don't have to just look like the guy whose butt's hangin' out. I take it as an honor now when people say we keep it clean.

At first it was, "You guys look kind of soft," or that wasn't expected of us. A black dude walked past the shop a couple days ago, he said, "You boys can't cut no hair," because culturally, black barbershops are typically hood. This is in Georgia. Because they don't know No Grease, thinking who these bourgeoisie-ass, who are these guys? But he saw these guys kept somebody in their chair, so they must know what they're doing. It's funny to see that now, going to another market and people not knowing you, because at first down there, the Latino clientele responded to us real quick. They were our first foundation in Georgia, so people when they walked by, the only thing they saw us cutting was Latinos or others, not blacks. I didn't know what to expect. I'm in Georgia so I'm gonna cut a lot of black people, that's what I'm thinking. Right by Atlanta. So when the Latino clientele responded to that, we just thought we'd cut a lot of Latinos. But then black people walking by saying, "Yo, you don't cut black people's hair? I'm black." That's like the rule of thumb, as a black barber, if nobody's hair we cut, we cut our hair. So to see that and that response, it was eye-opening.

Oddly, a lot of people think we're owned by white people. It's crazy. Black people have said it and white people have said it. It's the service, the quality, the presentation—everything is beyond people's expectations. Especially of a black business, a black barbershop. We go beyond what they're expecting, so they figure we can't be black owned. To us, presentation is signage, the colors on the wall, the art on the wall, the way the barbers are dressed, to the music being played. Even if you're just coming in to be nosy, you're going to be drawn. Remember, a barbershop is still a place of that socializing. We tell our barbers, "You need to read a book outside of this. If you're into sports, read about sports. I want you to know so much about sports that you can talk sports all day. If you wanna be somebody who reads the Bible, you need to read the Bible so you can talk scripture all day. But you need to be reading and make sure that you can talk and communicate on all different topics." You need to be a well-rounded man; you need to be different things. You need to read things you don't even know that you like. When you're in the barber business, you're liable to meet anybody. There's something about being well-versed. That kind of stuff is a must and you have to do it intentionally. The clients don't know. In the beginning stages, the barbers don't even know.

* * * * * *

One of the biggest hurdles for young black men is the impact of broken families. In many cases, they have difficulty with structure and roles. I see young men and older people who never had much structure or roles and so anything goes. And the only thing they're asking you either directly or indirectly is give me some structure. Give me some direction. I used to be afraid of that. I ain't your father; I ain't none of that. Yo, this is business. I don't want to be your daddy. I don't want to tell a grown-ass man what to do. But if you don't, that's why they came—they want that direction. It's a lot to take on. I can look at it personally, as someone who wants to help people and develop people. I know it's good for them; it makes me feel good. But then from the business side, I can build a business too. So it's a two-fold thing. I get the enjoyment of helping someone to make you feel good and I can build a business also.

Humility is a big thing, too. Those who come in and are humble, I know I can work with them. Because some come in with egos bigger than the world, with the cockiest, most competitive spirit, the crab-in-the-bucket mentality, and I can see that one too. I let them come in; we gonna put you in your proper place because we know you're gonna deal with that. More likely you're not gonna come with No Grease. We're gonna let the world take care of you. The big-head one, the big ego-head, that one comes in, he's got all the answers, he ain't never need anybody for nothing, nobody never did nothing for him, he got here on his own. "My momma didn't do nothing, my daddy didn't do nothing, nobody ever done nothing for me. I'm here." I say, "OK cool, man. We're gonna try to give you the tools that you need to become a better barber." But he'll be the one like, "I don't wanna work with No Grease," and I'm like nah nah because we're not gonna be able to do nothing for you. We let you go out there and let the world kick your ass. Because I know, the majority of most, especially black barbershops, don't have no structure. It's a Cowboys-and-Indians type of experience. You come in, you get high, you do whatever you want, you come in when you want, they'd never know. Once you get your ass kicked like that, it happens every time. A barber comes to our school; we don't take him as a barber with us for a lot of different reasons. Maybe he didn't want to be with us and we didn't want him. Or whatever. And he'll go out there but he got the skills. Damn, but if you only had some humility, you'd be that dude. You go out there and work for a couple years and I see him and he like, "You got anything open, man? I like y'all's structure, I like what you're doing. I like your image." Because now, ultimately, he wants some direction.

Because we're so connected, we're heightened to our sensitivities of each other. Because I grew up with you, I'm around you all the time, I know when you ain't feeling good, I know when something ain't right. If we don't have those experiences in our family, where are you going to get those experiences from? Ultimately, there's something good in all of us. I believe that. But if you don't have something to help them nurture that and develop that, you'll never see the best of us. That's what we've done: We've created something in the barber industry that gives our people something to navigate through, develop without being judged. Structure is key.

Most new barbers come in saying the only things they care about is getting paid. They say, "I've been broke all my life, I just need to make some money." They think money is the answer to everything, and so they're chasing the dollar. We provide a legitimate vehicle to get them the dollar. So with us understanding that, that's one of the first things I talk to a barber about. Because it ain't like a typical job; I don't just dish out salaries. I say, "What you trying to make?" And most of them will say something crazy. Somebody might say I just need to make $500 a week. And I'm like that's legit. In my mind, I know in my business, I can help you with that. Now the money thing is off the table. Now if you're gonna say $100,000 my first year, I'm gonna say, "Now, boy, you gonna cut some hair. It ain't gonna happen your first year, but this is the path to get you there."

If you got a path to dealing with the money issue, given especially men but even our female barbers, if you give them some type of assurance that they will be able to take care of themselves financially, they'll hear you say a lot of other stuff. If that ain't happening, it's done. We call it the 90-day rule. We got 90 days to show you your financial whatever, but you gotta show me in 90 days that you got what it takes. If I hold true to mine, you hold true to yours, you should get it. And that's how we hold each other accountable. I'm gonna do my part, you're gonna do your part, and we'll see the results. Of course, they start chasing the money for a couple years. Everybody wants to make as much possible money as they want. But what I've seen over the years if you haven't dealt with your habits and the things you need to deal with, you're just gonna multiply those things. So if you're spending your money on clothes, you're gonna multiply spending money on clothes. When you get them younger, it's a different conversation as opposed to when I'm talking to a thirty-, thirty-five-year-old man with a wife and kids. Then when you're talking to a man or woman on the other side of it, now they're doing it for retirement or just because they don't want to be home anymore, they just always wanted to cut hair. It's a different conversation, case by case.

I've seen values change through the years. With the younger cats, it used to be, "I wanna get married." That ain't what I've been seeing lately. Now it's like, I got a kid here, and I wanna make some more money. I wanna take care of my kid but I don't really want a wife. I got married at twenty-six because that's what was showed to us in my generation. Reaching the next level meant becoming a husband and father and taking care of your family. Now that's rare. When I tell people I've been married seventeen years, that's not even a realistic thing to them. Now these barbers are coming in, male and female, they're bringing their sons in and letting them watch them work amongst these other brotherly examples around them, but their parents aren't together. I don't know how this is all going to play out in another ten years. Because what I'm seeing is young men and females raising their children but separately. I'm not saying it's good or bad; I'm just saying it's different.

Our West Side shop, Mosaic, has always been special to me. We opened just a few years ago, but I think Mosaic is gonna end up being that pillar shop here in Charlotte. If I had to hang my hat on something, it would be that Mosaic shop, not our shop in Uptown, because Mosaic is in our community. I don't want to take anything away from Uptown and what that means for our brand, but because of the connection with Smith and the people. It was like bringing Gucci to Beatties Ford Road. People really embraced us. The truth is, we had to fight to go down to the arena. They didn't really want us there. Here, they're like, "We need y'all here." This one is one of the hearts of my journey.

MELVIN HERRING

To African-American male students seeking mentorship at Johnson C. Smith University, few scholars are more popular or revered than Dr. Melvin Herring, director of the university's Master of Social Work program. A highly sought-after speaker on cultural competence and training from the South Carolina National Association of Workers Conference to the Charlotte-Mecklenburg Police Department, Dr. Herring earned a bachelor's degree from North Carolina A&T State University, a master's degree from the University of North Carolina at Charlotte, and a doctorate from the University of North Carolina at Greensboro. Along with recruiting and teaching at JCSU, Dr. Herring also shepherds master's level research and fosters ties with other universities, community organizations, programs, and external funding sources.

TEN MEN

Not long ago during my class, we discussed the Charlotte riots. This was critical because if you heard about protestors and rioters in the national media, you got an inaccurate impression. The reality was that there weren't just black people in the crowd, but white, Latino, gay, straight, disabled. People had connected their oppressions, which is always a powerful thing. When people connect oppressions, they can move mountains.

My students often ask, "Why can't the African-American community do what we did during Civil Rights? We have more technology now, but it's harder for us to get together." During the Civil Rights movement, you have two hundred people show up just from a flyer being passed out. What I tell them is, during the Civil Rights movement, we connected oppression, we connected pain. It didn't matter if you were rich, light-skinned, dark-skinned, poor, black—you were treated the same and you felt the same pain. When you connect pains, it's easier to connect people to move and do things. We've disconnected from our pain in the community. An educated black man tells himself he doesn't experience some of the stuff that some of my brothers here in the Northwest Corridor experience. When the time comes to fight, if I don't feel that pain, is it even in my best interest to go down there and fight? But what you saw in the protests Uptown was people connecting pains. And I believe we're going to see more and more of this.

There's a lot of ambiguity around situations like police shootings, particularly in the discipline of our profession, social work. By nature and by profession we want to help people and help change systems—that's just what we do as social workers. But you can't separate your ethnicity and all of the experiences that come along with that, so most of our students being of African-American descent, they have this ambiguity about even going into these systems. An experience like this says to them, "How do I help folk when I'm a victim of these same systems?" When the Keith Lamont Scott shooting first happened, we spent a lot of time in my class processing how they juxtapose their personal experiences besides their professional duties and responsibilities. We spent time on what does it really mean for us as an African-American community to experience what we experience collectively and vicariously through that situation? At the same time, how do we use that to help change the system and not allow that to be a barrier or resistance to changing the system?

Shortly after the incident, we held a community forum here at Smith's campus in collaboration with UNC Charlotte and the National Association of Social Workers for North Carolina. We brought in students, educators, practitioners in the social work profession to talk what change looks like among social workers of various identities, race, gender. So how do we really help folk when I don't even really know or have the same lens as a white social worker at UNC Charlotte? But we're working within the same profession with the same boundaries and principles. We started a dialogue here and we just had our second event and held it at UNC Charlotte about a month ago. Our goal is to continue to build on that, to really help get out into our profession and our community and our students to help lay a blueprint or foundation for how they address and handle issues like this moving forward.

Our students today are mostly millennials. This is an important demographic shift in America and in understanding how the technological advancement is changing how our kids see the world. This generation has the ability to have real-time feedback in terms of technology, seeing things as they happen—it's changing how they view the world. So a young white male in America now is able to see everything that happens to my son, your son, and vice versa, so it's really changing the landscape of how information is being passed on to this generation, which changes how they see the world.

TEN MEN

When we were growing up, in order for us to know an experience that happened to someone else, that information had to literally be transferred or conveyed from someone who saw that or that person themselves. You don't have to have that right now. You can do something and not even know that thing is being transferred or conveyed immediately to everybody. So I don't need to wait on your version of the story; I get to see it instantly. And that's totally changing how they see the world.

The millennials are just different than us. Their ideology is different, and different isn't bad. Everything they do is mostly limited including social interaction. Social interaction is more technologically engaged, and driven by more real-time information. So they make it work for them. They have major conversations sitting in their room with one little device, and they're talking to twenty different people. It's their version of what would have been our house party or social at someone's house where everyone gets together. They don't have to do that anymore, and it makes inclusion a little bit easier for them. The sharing of information is easier with them, which is a promising development.

Here's what I mean. You have an African-American kid at a predominately white school, and that kid experiences some form of overt racism. What happens now, as opposed to our generations, is that when that happens, a white student will say, "Wait a minute, that's wrong." Or it might be a gay kid who's experiencing some kind of bullying and a straight kid or heterosexual kid will say, "That's wrong." Because that's the progressive nature of acceptance and inclusion is so much stronger than what ours was. And that's innately connected to their ability to have real-time information all the same. So they're seeing these elements of things just being wrong and it's different from how I'm experiencing the world and they understand that's different, that's wrong. It's happening all over; it could be on the job and you see a woman get passed over. For the younger generation, a young man isn't going to have the same reaction as an older male would. They would be like, "Wait a minute, why didn't she get that job?"

Just think about the nature of what's happening. This generation is recognizing that the system has some type of barrier embedded within it that creates resistance to a particular identity. And they are recognizing it in real time so that the more they witness these resistances, the more they say this is wrong. They can see it happening all over and say, "We gotta change this." Hence you have a protest like you saw down in Charlotte, where you have this multi-racial, multi-faceted group in terms of social identities marching for this cause that fifteen years ago would have been viewed as black-white or a black thing.

Many of our systems and institutions are changing with this generation and that's okay too. Take, for instance, the institutions of marriage and family. When you talk about the family unit as a system, that has always been something of a fallacy. The nuclear family never really was the reality in our America. That may be how we promote it, but it's never been the case. Dysfunction has always been a part of the family unit. I think what's happening now is we just get to see the dysfunction up close and personal because of demographic shifts and technology.

* * * * * *

The notion of the black male being endangered isn't overblown; it's a very real issue for not just the black community, but in our community at large. Part of it I think is internal and part of it is systemic. There are things that we as black men have to shift and change, like for one the conveying of information from generation to generation. We used to have the platform of

TEN MEN

I'm sitting at grandpa's knee and he's sharing his stories, or if like me, you came from a single-parent home, my uncles and aunts or my brothers—they were the ones who conveyed that information. But we don't have those platforms anymore. Ask yourself how often do you have the time with your own sons at the level that we were able to do back in the day because we have the sense of urgency about all these other things we have to get done and the use of technology that creates a further divide in social interaction. We need to understand that that's how we were raised, but for this generation, this is their medium and we need to reach out through their mediums.

When we grew up we saw what was right in front of us, so if my dad was a mechanic, that's what I saw—him being a mechanic coming home in grease. Mother too, whatever my mother did, that's what I saw. Kids today get to see astronauts on the moon literally, immediately, so their conceptual universe is so much broader than ours. I would be sadly mistaken to think my son is going to follow in my trajectory right now, because he has so much at his doorstep, so much he sees so often. We spent a lot of time watching TV; they spend even more time in these mediums, they see so much, they know they have options.

We have the information to guide them—we don't know how to connect with them to guide them. That's where I see the big disconnect. I haven't seen a father yet who can't articulate what they think is best for their son or daughter to move forward in life to be a successful adult. The problem is how to convey that to them. That's where the disconnect is. That's what we have to be able to do. The ownership is on us to move into their space. The ownership isn't on them to say, "Can you please come and show me?" That's not where it is because me, as a thirteen-, fourteen-, fifteen-year-old kid, I wasn't raising my hand asking anyone to show me anything. It just happened to be right there in front of me. It's just different. We can't look at what we did as being right or wrong; it just was. We can't look at what they're doing as being right or wrong; it just is. We have to immerse ourselves in their culture. That's what inclusion is all about—immersing yourself into things that are different from what you're accustomed to.

I think we're so rooted into how we learned and did things, but a big thing—and this is across racial lines—men in general, we need to be able to rethink how we perceive our masculinity and machismo. That's a big thing. When I was growing up, I do something wrong, Daddy's gonna punch me in the chest. "Get it right, boy!" That kind of mindset. To bring a child to sit down and just have a conversation to explore the child's thinking, that's not manly, that's not how to show him; you do it. This generation of males is different because they do everything, I think, in a less masculine, as we would perceive it, approach. We have to be able to say, "In order to reach this kid, I am willing to go to this level."

There's confusion among these young guys because they know the way they function and operate within the context of their peers, but then they see the other men, older men, doing this physical thing and it's confusing to them. They don't know how to integrate the two. Even something as simple as talking. For the young guys, or their generation generally, they don't sit down and talk much because technology increases that social interaction gap. We need to be able to communicate through their means. I text my son all the time. It's easier for me to pick up the phone and call him if I need something, and that's what most men do. We think: I ain't sitting here taking the time to type up all this—I'm gonna call him. But through me texting my son, he gets used to hearing my voice through text. That's a powerful thing that people don't get. When someone sends you a text, you get to start in your mind, the schema in your mind. Because of your experiences with that person, their voice, their mannerisms, you begin to read people's texts based on what you know about them. That same thing is happening with my son. He has his social interactions with me, so if I send him a text, he can identify the context in how I'm saying something through text, another language. He hears my voice when he reads my text. But if you're never texting, that means you're probably limiting your conversations with your kids because that's the way they communicate.

The way our lives are structured now, we don't have as much time to be around our kids the way we did growing up. So if you're waiting to have social, actual verbal conversations with your kids, you're limiting how much time you can have with your kids. It's important, very important. And that's how we get this next generation of black men to start seeing and understanding. I monitor my kids' emails. I don't go through their phones or whatever because it's a level of trust until they gotta give me a reason not to, but little boys are communicating to little girls now through text messaging and Snapchat and these social media outlets.

That's where they live. If we don't go live there with them, there's such a thing in the literature called psychological absence, particularly around fathers. Psychological absence is as damaging as physical absence and can be more damaging at times. If we're talking about a father who's there but never connects with their child emotionally, always kind of distant in terms of their interaction with the kid, cold, versus the father who doesn't live in the household, a non-residential father, who every time they get a chance to be with their child is very loving, holding, embracing, just totally open. Research shows that that non-residential father is going to have more of a positive impact on their child than that father who's there in the home but psychologically distant.

I think that's part of the dysfunction men rarely ever talk about. The literature talks about the resiliency in the kids, that you're able to experience this psychological disconnection in many ways, but there's something about the kids that are able to accept and understand and move forward positively. But resiliency is like DNA; it's different for everybody. If you took a group of older men and asked them about their relationships with their fathers, I would be willing to bet that if you got a hundred of those together that said yeah, their father was the kind who, though he loved them, came home and never really talked. We have to do better than our fathers at communicating. We are creating a space for even residential fathers to be psychologically absent. It's unintentional. That's why, every day in many mediums, I tell my son, "Love you, man."

Daniel Wallace Culp enrolled at Biddle Memorial Institute (now Johnson C. Smith University) in 1869, and in 1876 became among its first graduates. *Photographer unknown/Courtesy of the Inez Moore Parker Archives at Johnson C. Smith University. All Rights Reserved.*

Blacksmithing students train at Biddle University in the early 1900s. *Photographer unknown/JCSU Archives/Courtesy of Robinson-Spangler Carolina Room, Public Library of Charlotte and Mecklenburg County.*

Groundskeepers on Biddle University campus. *Photographer unknown/Courtesy of the Inez Moore Parker Archives at Johnson C. Smith University. All Rights Reserved.*

The Print Shop at Biddle University in 1914. *Photographer unknown/JCSU Archives/Courtesy of Robinson-Spangler Carolina Room, Public Library of Charlotte and Mecklenburg County.*

A group of Biddle University graduates, class of 1916. *Photographer unknown/Courtesy of the Inez Moore Parker Archives at Johnson C. Smith University. All Rights Reserved.*

Dr. Hardy Liston, president of JCSU from 1947-1956, with Jackie Robinson, the first African American to play in Major League Baseball. *Photographer unknown/Courtesy of the Inez Moore Parker Archives at Johnson C. Smith University. All Rights Reserved.*

JCSU swim team. *Photographer unknown/Courtesy of the Inez Moore Parker Archives at Johnson C. Smith University. All Rights Reserved.*

Biddle University football team in front of Carnegie Hall in 1917. *Photographer unknown/Courtesy of the Inez Moore Parker Archives at Johnson C. Smith University. All Rights Reserved.*

Biddle University's first basketball team in front of Carnegie Library in 1917. *Photographer unknown/ Courtesy of the Inez Moore Parker Archives at Johnson C. Smith University. All Rights Reserved.*

January 13, 1968 - Dr. Reginald Hawkins, a local dentist and Charlotte civil rights stalwart, resided in the McCrorey Heights neighborhood, one of Charlotte's oldest black, middle-class neighborhoods. Hawkins was the first African American to run for governor in North Carolina since Reconstruction. *Photographer unknown/Courtesy of The Charlotte Observer.*

JCSU students (from right) Robert Hunt, Joan Adams Siler, Ann Frazier Walker and Virginia Lee protest at a Charlotte lunch counter on Feb. 11, 1960. *Photographer unknown/Courtesy of Robinson-Spangler Carolina Room, Public Library of Charlotte and Mecklenburg County.*

Charles Jones, a member of the Freedom Riders, talks about student protests to reporters in February 1960. *Photographer unknown/Courtesy of The Charlotte Observer.*

Charles Jones (right) urges peace and civility among JCSU students sitting in at Woolworth's lunch counter in Charlotte February 9, 1960. *Photographer unknown/Courtesy of The Charlotte Observer.*

West Charlotte High School Photography Club in 1957. *Photographer unknown/Courtesy of West Charlotte High School.*

West Charlotte High School basketball team, 1951 yearbook. *Photographer unknown/ Courtesy of West Charlotte High School.*

The Junior Band at West Charlotte High School in 1943. *Photographer unknown/Courtesy of Robinson-Spangler Carolina Room, Public Library of Charlotte and Mecklenburg County.*

West Charlotte High School Hi-Y club, a Y.M.C.A. (Young Men's Christian Association) social club, in 1965. *Photographer unknown/Courtesy of West Charlotte High School.*

The Excelsior Club was a popular social hub on Beatties Ford Road for African Americans before integration. *Photographer unknown/Courtesy of Robinson-Spangler Carolina Room, Public Library of Charlotte and Mecklenburg County.*

Excelsior Club Board of Directors in 1944. Left to right: Reuben McKissick, Samuel Moore, Harry Mills, Harry Plater, Arthur Bass, Roy Perry. Photo courtesy of Minnie McKee. *Photographer unknown/Courtesy of Robinson-Spangler Carolina Room, Public Library of Charlotte and Mecklenburg County.*

Churchgoers gather in front of Jane E. Smith Memorial Church after a service. *Photographer unknown/Courtesy of the Inez Moore Parker Archives at Johnson C. Smith University. All Rights Reserved.*

Dr. Roy S. Wynn, Charlotte's first black ophthalmologist, opened his office in 1941. Wynn, the first black African American to serve on the board of the Charlotte Housing Authority, resided in Oaklawn, one of Charlotte's historic black neighborhoods. *Photographer unknown/Courtesy of Robinson-Spangler Carolina Room, Public Library of Charlotte and Mecklenburg County.*

JCSU graduate Damian Johnson, co-founder of men's hair care company, No Grease Inc., and client Bob Johnson, BET founder. *Photo by Danjon Meredith/ Courtesy of Damian Johnson.*

From left to right: James "Smuggie" Mitchell, JCSU president Dr. Ronald L. Carter, Jermaine Johnson, Damian Johnson, David Howard, Harold Cogdell and Charlie Petty during the grand opening of No Grease at Mosaic Village in April 2013. *Photo by Danjon Meredith/Courtesy of Damian Johnson.*

Cedric Mangum, right, one of Charlotte's best-known House Of Prayer bandleaders, leads "shout" musicians in a jam session outside the United House of Prayer for All People on Beatties Ford Road in 2008. *Photo by T. Ortega Gaines/Courtesy of The Charlotte Observer.*

Mourners gather for the funeral of late civil rights attorney Julius Chambers at Friendship Missionary Baptist Church Thursday, August 8, 2013. *Photo by Todd Sumlin/Courtesy of The Charlotte Observer.*

JCSU students rally following the police shooting death of Keith Lamont Scott shooting in September 2016. *Photo by Joshua Nypaver/Johnson C. Smith University.*

JCSU students protest the police shooting death of Keith Lamont Scott shooting in September 2016. *Photo by Joshua Nypaver/Johnson C. Smith University.*

Charles Jones reminisces with youth about his experiences as an original Freedom Rider. *Photo by Robert Lahser/Courtesy of The Charlotte Observer.*

Colin Pinkney, a grassroots community leader, mentors African-American male students through his Young Male Book Club. *Photo by Diedra Laird/Courtesy of The Charlotte Observer.*

Members of the Biddleville-Smallwood Neighborhood Association gather at Smallwood Presbyterian Church for their monthly meeting. *Photo by Jeff Siner/Courtesy of The Charlotte Observer.*

Biddleville-Smallwood Neighborhood Association president Elliott Hipp, left, takes notes as treasurer Rico Mungo, right, addresses residents at Smallwood Presbyterian Church. *Photo by Jeff Siner/Courtesy of The Charlotte Observer.*

Bishop Claude Richard Alexander Jr., senior pastor at The Park Church on Beatties Ford Road (formally University Park Baptist Church), calls the congregation to the altar for a blessing. *Photo by Tyrus Ortega Gaines.*

Darryl Gaston, community activist and pastor of Smallwood Presbyterian Church. *Photo by Austin Caine.*

Charlotte Hornets' Ricky Davis (left) and CMPD Sgt. Spencer Cochran (right) deliver a Thanksgiving dinner to Tawanna Gregory. *Photo by David T. Foster III/Courtesy of The Charlotte Observer.*

Greg Pappanastos (left), owner of Savona Mill, discusses a proposed trolley line with T'Afo Feimster, an arts and culture educator, and J'Tanya Adams, founder and president of Historic West End Partners. *Photo by John D. Simmons/Courtesy of The Charlotte Observer.*

Charlotte artist Tommie Robinson completes a set of murals at the old Friendship Missionary Baptist Church. *Photo by Tyrus Ortega Gaines/Courtesy of The Charlotte Observer.*

Local artist Abel Jackson works on a mural of the Underground Railroad displayed at Mosaic Village. *Photo by T'Afo Feimster.*

Darrel Williams, right, celebrates the 20th anniversary of his architectural firm, Neighboring Concepts. *Photo by Jon Strayhorn.*

JAMES PEELER

In 1954, amidst the U.S. Supreme Court's landmark ruling banning
segregation in public schools, one of Charlotte's native sons returned home
to a city bitterly divided. James Gibson Peeler, a graduate of West Charlotte
High School and Johnson C. Smith University, had served in the Army
during the Korean War before moving to New York to study photography at
the New York Institute of Photography. Upon arriving in Charlotte, Peeler
opened a photography studio on Beatties Ford Road, and for the next 50
years would become perhaps the city's most important documentarians of
African-American life and culture. As a kind of Gordon Parks of his day,
Peeler's voluminous portfolio includes images that not only capture Charlotte's
day-to-day black experience, from weddings to baptisms to school dances,
but also such historic events as civil rights marches of the Rev. Martin Luther
King, the Freedom Rides, and the sit-in movement. Over the past few years,
archivists at JCSU have been working to preserve thousands of images rescued
after a fire destroyed Peeler's studio in 2003, and graciously have permitted
us to publish several images in this volume. The following pages offer a rare
glimpse at historic black Charlotte through the late Peeler's extraordinary lens.

Images used courtesy of the James Peeler Collection,
Inez Moore Parker Archives, Johnson C. Smith University.

© James Peeler

© James Peeler

© James Peeler

© James Peeler

© James Peeler

© James Peeler

© James Peeler

© James Peeler

© James Peeler

© James Peeler

© James Peeler

© James Peeler

DARREL WILLIAMS

For nearly three decades, Darrel Williams, Sr., FAIA, has proven to be a major force in Charlotte, an architect with vision and heart. A founding partner of Neighboring Concepts, Williams's stock-in-trade is bridging the gap between the physical and social challenges facing urban communities. Among Williams's strengths is his insight into Charlotte's challenges as a growing city, gleaned during four consecutive terms on the Mecklenburg County Board of Commissioners, and extending into work in civic and community organizations, from the Charlotte-Mecklenburg Library Board of Trustees to the boards of Central Piedmont Community College, Charlotte Mecklenburg Library Foundation, The Nature Conservancy, and various others. A native of Baton Rouge, Williams has been a key voice and visionary behind the overall revitalization of the Northwest Corridor, recently relocating his own firm to West Trade Street near Johnson C. Smith University.

TEN MEN

I grew up in Baton Rouge, Louisiana, in a family in which all the males were brick masons. My father, grandfather, uncles and cousins older than me were all brick masons. I grew up in various low-income communities in the Baton Rouge area where I stumbled into the architecture profession. No one in my family had attended college. I'm the second oldest of seven children. Of the seven of us, my youngest brother and I were the only two to attend college. We both graduated from Southern University in Baton Rouge. Up through seventh grade I had attended all-black schools.

Prior to my eighth-grade year, schools integrated in Louisiana, so in eighth grade, we were sort of thrown in the mix to attend white schools for the first time, not knowing what to expect or anticipate. The white students did not want us at their schools and we did not care to be there. Dealing with racist issues and doing things we shouldn't have been doing and getting into trouble were the norm for several of my friends and I. We survived junior high school and went on to attend the senior high school, which was integrated as well, while experiencing the same challenges.

If we didn't get any encouragement at home to go to college, we surely didn't get it at school. The counselors, obviously with no diversity training, saw all of us young black boys as problems. They could not imagine us going to college, so they didn't encourage or help prepare us to attend. As a consequence, I graduated from high school and the only math I had taken was general math. I did not take algebra or other courses required to attend college. I did take several art and drafting courses which I really enjoyed. Several of us were often getting into trouble and getting put out of school.

Due to the environment I grew up in and the negative things I was exposed to, along with my immaturity, I fathered two sons before marriage, one prior to finishing high school and the other prior to graduating from college. My first son was ten years old before I accepted my responsibility as a parent. The excuse I used was, I wasn't sure he was my son.

While in high school, oftentimes, several of my friends and I would crash house parties on weekends. After meeting a young lady who lived at the last house party I crashed, it changed my life. She was different than anyone I had known relative to her background and her desire to attend college after high school. While in the eleventh grade, she knew she was going to be attending college on a physics scholarship. Obviously, she was very smart and having an uncle and aunt who were professors on Southern University campus were an obvious influence. As we started dating, I started thinking more and more about my future in lieu of the negative path I was taking. Needless to say, she inspired me to start thinking about attending college. Even though Southern University was only about two miles from where I was growing up, I had no intention of going to college until I met her.

A few guys from my neighborhood were attending Southern University. When I started thinking about attending college, coincidentally, I was wandering around campus one day and ran into a brother from my neighborhood who graduated high school a year before me. He was majoring in architecture and he invited me to his studio lab on campus. While visiting his studio, I was so fascinated with the work they were doing, I decided to do some research on architecture. After understanding that architecture was directly related to art and drafting (what I had been enjoying in high school) and construction (what I had been exposed to all my life), I decided then that I wanted to become an architect.

Seeing how hard my father, grandfather, uncles, and cousins had to work to make a living in the cold, rain, and hot, humid summers of Louisiana, I knew that I did not want to be a brick mason. Prior to going on campus and going to my friend's studio, I was thinking more about attending an art school and becoming an artist. My mother could draw anything better than anyone I knew, so she inspired me to want to draw, which is why I took several art classes in high school.

Once I decided that I wanted to attend Southern University and major in architecture, I checked into it and found out that I had not taken all the courses I should have in high school to enroll in college. I was told that to major in architecture, I would have to take all the courses that I should have taken in high school as well as the other courses needed for an architecture major. Unlike several other majors, a Bachelor in Architecture degree was a five-year program and you start architecture classes during the first year. Had I been required to take an admission test to enroll in college, I would have never had the opportunity to attend because I just wasn't prepared. Due to my family financial situation, I was able to apply and receive a basic opportunity grant which paid 100 percent of my tuition each year. Without the grant or Southern University allowing me to double up on several classes to catch up, I would have never had the opportunity to attend college.

After enrolling in the architecture program, taking some classes and getting serious about school, it was then I realized that I had potential that I didn't know I had. I was never the smartest person in my class, but I did work harder than everyone else. I was truly inspired because for the first time in my life, I was very excited about school and the idea of studying to become an architect. As an architecture major, we would stay up two or three nights without sleeping working on our projects. I recall more than once placing tissue in my nose to keep my nose from bleeding while trying to finish my work. While growing up as a child, my nose always bled easy. It was always my way of skipping grade school when I didn't want to go.

During my college years, I was always very shy, lacking self-esteem. I didn't care for speaking in front of groups or doing a lot of talking. After the completion of our projects, to get a grade, we would have to present our work in front of professors or what we called a jury. When my classmates would finish their projects, I would keep drawing more and more until my drawings could explain my project. I would have my drawings popping off the paper so I wouldn't have to talk a whole lot. Some of my classmates would spend very little time drawing and could mesmerize the jury by just talking, but I could not do that. After five years in the architecture program, I graduated the most outstanding student in my class.

* * * * * *

As I indicated earlier, I made several mistakes in high school and while in college. The girl who I had met at the house party and inspired me to attend college, we dated off and on during college since high school. In addition to the son who was born while I was in high school, I made the same mistake again before graduating from college. After fathering my second son by a different girl, I realized I was headed down the wrong path once again. She wanted to get married and I wasn't interested so she married someone else. Even though I made an effort, I did not get to know my second son until after his mother was divorced when he was about twelve years old.

Consequently, I got back together with the girl who inspired me to attend college and we got married one week after graduation. I graduated one week, the next week I'm married to my high school sweetheart, and we moved to Denver where I got my first architectural job out of college. About three years later, we had our first son. Meanwhile, I was in denial and never really knew for sure or found out if my first son was really my son or not. While in Denver, my family back home gave me a hard time saying he was my son, but I wasn't sure because I hadn't seen him since he was very young.

After leaving Denver and moving to Charlotte, five years later, I was definitely more mature and began wondering, "What if he is my son?" I began to think about the environment that he was growing up in, which is where I grew up. I often wondered, what if something happens to him and he is my son? So I went home specifically to see him. And when I saw him, all I could do was cry. I knew right then that he was my son so we hugged and I just cried. Fortunately, my wife was compassionate and kind enough to say he could come live with us which was also approved by his mom. By then, he was ten years old, so I had a one-year-old son with my wife, a five-year-old with his mom and her husband and a ten-year-old.

A few years later, when my second son was about twelve years old, his mom and her husband divorced, which is when I started to get to know him. A few years later, my wife and I had another son, my youngest. Fortunately, I get along very well with all of my boys who have graduated from college and are married. Despite how we got here, I'm very proud of all my boys and they tell me that they are proud of me. My first wife and I divorced and I've been married to my second wife for almost fifteen years now. She has been a true blessing to me, helping me become a much better person than I was before I met her.

* * * * * *

In 1994, I had the opportunity to become a Mecklenburg County Commissioner in which I was elected for four consecutive terms. Being in elected office wasn't something that I desired or had planned to do. When we arrived in Charlotte in 1983, I was still very shy with low self-esteem. A few years later, a white friend and fellow architect asked if I would be willing to become a charter member of a new all-white Optimist Club in Charlotte. The motto for Optimist Clubs is "Friend of Youth," helping kids become all they can be. At the time, First Ward was called Earle Village, one of Charlotte's most challenging public housing developments at the time.

Of course, with all the white guys involved and with my low self-esteem, I was very reluctant but decided to join because of the thought of working with kids. As a club, all of our early work was within the Earle Village public housing complex. Since I was the only black member, I felt obligated to be involved in everything we did. When I saw those little kids running around Earle Village, I saw myself. In addition to taking leadership classes and joining a Toastmasters Club, working with those kids was the single most important thing that had me feeling real good about myself and helped to build my self-esteem. I began to really believe that I can make a difference in the lives of young people. Later, our club started a Junior Optimist Club in Earle Village, which caused me to become even more involved in working with the kids and helping them to believe they could be anything they wanted to be.

My family and I lived in Third Ward close to our community park, Frazier Park, which runs adjacent to and parallel to I-77. Prior to the merger of the City and County parks departments, during the time, most of the parks within the city limits were deplorable and Frazier Park was no exception. Every time I visited the park with my kids, I would get very frustrated because of the old rusted playground equipment. After my persistence of complaining and sharing photos with City Council members, including our Councilman, former State Senator Charlie Dannelly. After Councilman Dannelly got tired of me complaining, he appointed me to the City Parks Advisory Committee. A few years later following the merger of the City and County parks departments, I joined the Mecklenburg County Parks Commission.

Later, I became a member of Mecklenburg County Housing and Development Committee. This committee was responsible for helping the County Housing Department improve housing and infrastructure conditions for residents who lived within the unincorporated areas of the County. Residents in some of these areas did not have water and sewer and lived in substandard housing conditions. We had a hard time getting County Commissioners to visit these areas, so we spent a lot of time making videotapes to show the Commissioners how some of these residents were living.

After about a year and a half of being in Charlotte, I was very fortunate to join the firm of Gantt Huberman Architects (GHA) as a young architect where I worked for almost twelve years prior to starting my own firm. In addition to reviving my career as an architect, working at GHA was very inspiring relative to the opportunity to give back to the community through volunteerism. Often times, Mayor Gantt would speak to young architects about how our training as architects could help shape public policy.

In 1993, I received a call from a member of the Democratic Party about seeking a new seat that was being created in a new district for the Mecklenburg Board of County Commissioners. My initial reaction was, there was no way I was getting involved in politics. However, after doing some research and gaining a better understanding of the role the County Commissioners had in our community, I began thinking about the possibility. Particularly when I realized that the issues I had been focusing on and fighting for during the past several years were funded by the County Commissioners.

When it became clear to me that this was something I needed to do, I started losing sleep at night. After not making things happen fast enough while serving on advisory boards, I felt some obligation to keep fighting. It was then I went to Harvey Gantt and his partner, Jeffrey Huberman, to seek their advice and discuss the possibility of running for a seat on the Board of County Commissioners. To my surprise, they strongly encouraged me to run so I had no more excuses. The firm promoted a culture of giving back to the community, so I should not have been surprised. At that point, I just didn't have any excuses anymore. They were the first to write me checks for my campaign.

I gravitated toward parks so much because where I grew up, we didn't have nice parks. All we had was a basketball court with rocks projecting out of the pavement. Because of my background and my experiences as a Parks Commissioner, it was very obvious to me that better parks and recreation facilities are essential to helping keep young people out of trouble, particularly in our urban communities. In 1994, I won my election and served four consecutive terms. During my term on the County Commission, I was able to influence the budget and ensure that Parks and Recreation and my other interests such as improving substandard housing conditions and infrastructure in our unincorporated areas had adequate resources.

The same thing that keeps me from being just another architect brings me back to the Northwest Corridor. We have enough architects who would prefer to work in areas of our community where there are very few problems and challenges. Despite my circumstances growing up, God connected me with the right people in my life at the right time, which allowed me to become an elected official and architect so that I can help improve the kind of communities that I grew up in. Not to become just another architect but to discover my purpose and help improve our most socially and physically challenged urban communities. Why would I have stumbled into this profession, become an elected official, and started a firm, Neighboring Concepts, to focus on transforming communities through architecture? I feel very blessed to have found my purpose and the opportunity to work with other professionals in our firm who are as passionate as I am about what we do each and every day.

TEN MEN

After working with former Superior Court Judge Shirley Fulton to develop an implementation plan to revitalize the Historic Wesley Heights neighborhood, my partners and I attempted to develop an old dilapidated historic building on West Morehead. Despite being in a city with tremendous resources and banking, we were told that we were on the wrong side of the interstate. Now, the West Morehead area is a thriving area of our community with new developments announced, new businesses and restaurants, a place where others want to be.

However, we understood planning and development well enough to know that it's too close to a thriving Center City that if the city kept growing, eventually that growth would expand to the west. Now that West Morehead is thriving, Neighboring Concepts has relocated our office to the West Trade Street area, now called Historic West End. Coincidentally, we are back near Johnson C. Smith University campus where the firm was started over twenty years ago. Historic West End will be revitalized and become a thriving, diverse, and walkable community with wonderful places to live, work, and play while promoting the culture and history of the entire area.

TITUS IVORY

Among the most exciting developments at West Charlotte High School in re-cent years was the hiring of Titus Ivory as its athletic director. Ivory is a former basketball and football star at rival North Mecklenburg, but his family boasts a rich legacy of achievement at West Charlotte—which Ivory intends to restore to its former glory. His late father, Titus Sr., was a legendary athlete at West Charlotte. Ivory brings lot of experience to his new role. After playing basketball for Penn State, he spent more than a decade as a pro overseas in Italy, Germany, Belgium, Israel, the Philippines, and Lithuania, where he won two European League na-tional championships and a German Cup title.

TEN MEN

When I first got this job, it was rough. Everybody wanted to pray for me. I was like, why does everybody want to pray for me? Within a few weeks, I began to understand why. I mean, I was getting cussed out by kids—hardcore cussed out. I was like, "Who are you talking to? Me?" I couldn't believe it. I witnessed disrespect in ways that I just didn't think kids had the audacity to do.

I knew it was a trust issue. It was, "Who are you? I don't know who you are, so I can't respect you yet. I don't know you. I can do this to you, talk to you this way, because I do it to everybody." They felt entitled to behave as though, "I don't know who you are, so I'm gonna treat you like I treat everybody else in the neighborhood. You're a teacher, but you're not my teacher." And even at the gym, it was like, "I'm not even in your class, so why are you talkin' to me?"

My position was, "Well, I'm the athletic director, I'm an administrator in a gymnasium, so if I say, 'Put it away,' if I say, 'Sit down,' 'Do this,' 'Stop cussing,' then you should be able to do that. I may not be not your teacher right now, but I am a supervisor in this gymnasium and you will respect me." The good news is that slowly, things have gotten better. Once the students got to know me, the attitudes started to change, and a lot of the opposition has tapered off. But honestly, it takes time.

When I arrived, one thing that was instantly clear was that the kids here today don't know the rich history here at West Charlotte. This was a school of high prestige, high honor. It has historical value. But that message has gotten lost over time. You have the kids in the neighborhood who don't really understand what our legacy means or what that represents. Many of them don't have involved fathers, a lot of them are growing up in single-parent households. I won't blame all of it on this, but you can't help but ask: who are your role models? Who are the people you're looking up to?

The other truth is that much of what kids learn today is from the internet.

TITUS IVORY

They live in a microwave culture, where instant gratification, instant success, instant popularity is in their hands. I teach them that internet cuts both ways; if it's negative, it can hurt you. If it's positive, it can bring some type of value to you. I tell them every day, "As much as y'all are on that phone or that internet, let's put some positive things out there. Let's do something to change the world in a positive way." The first thing some kids want to do is pick up their phone and tape a fight and post it everywhere. Instead of stopping their friend from fighting, they want to see it and view it over and over again.

There's another hard truth: we've lost a lot of strong families from the neighborhood over the past couple of decades. Many of the most affluent, influential families who provided a strong foundation for young people have moved out of the neighborhood. Sometimes it feels as though many of the adults have lost faith in our young people, in helping them set their priorities straight and achieve the goals.

So the challenge for me has been introducing the kids to the West Charlotte that I know, respect and love. To bring the lion and the roar back to West Charlotte. It's a process, but we're well underway. I've gotten some new coaches to come over here, and I've brought some inspirational speakers to the school. I've brought people here who have the same spiritual values and foundation that I have. Mostly, I'm trying to get coaches to understand that you have to teach these kids about what life is, to share their testimonies and provide them with a road map that will allow them to successfully navigate their lives.

* * * * * *

When I started here, one of the first things I did was hang my dad's West Charlotte basketball jersey on my office wall. I put it up there for a reason: to show my heritage and the heritage of this school to students. Not only did my dad go to high school here, but so did my grandmother, my aunts and my uncles. My aunt taught here. I went to North Meck, and my North Meck hat is up there, too, but I have a legacy at this school. I have people say, "You gotta get that hat out of here, Coach." But that's who I am. Still, I realize that I have more heritage here at West Charlotte.

Even at North Meck, my experience at West Charlotte shaped much of my character. When I came to compete against West Charlotte, I knew that I was in for a dogfight. When I walked through this gymnasium, or when I walked out on that field, I knew that it wasn't going to be an easy win, if it was a win at all. So I was fearful, but I understood I had to come compete. Some of my teammates said, "I just wanna get out of here." Because to them, there was an aura around this school.

The year before my senior year, '94, West Charlotte went to the state championship. And then in '95, they went back to the state championship and won it. So during my three years of playing football, West Charlotte was a powerhouse, to the point where I'm a defensive back, I'm off the line like twenty yards, and they're still blowin' by me. That's the caliber of student athletes that this school produced. In basketball, my junior year, we beat them to go to Hickory in the Final Four. The rivalry between the schools was fierce. The prestige, price, and competitiveness around this school is what I'm trying to get these kids to understand and appreciate.

I spent eleven years working in basketball overseas, so I've seen youth culture in other countries, I've seen other how young people aspire to be Americans and aspire to be young people here, but our kids aren't aware just how much how they are envied and admired around the world. They don't know what's outside of Beatties Ford Road. All they know is, "What I put on social media, nobody's gonna mess with me, I've got my homeboys going to back me up, I need to live for today." In some cases, that's understandable because a lot of our kids do grow up in hard circumstances. There are kids living in cars who aren't getting anything to eat except for at school. It's a reality. So when kids come back to school every day and they have a situation, I try to address it in a constructive way. "Tell me what's going on," and I try to help them.

When you ask kids, "What is your objective at the high school?" "Coach, I want to go to Yale. I wanna go to college. I wanna get a successful job. I wanna have money." I tell them that in order to do those things, you need you to be successful in school right now. We need you to understand that you have to cope with all the adversities that you're surrounded with and you gotta deal with it in a positive way. You can't cuss out a teacher. You can't go around fighting people. You gotta build a reputation for yourself so that down the line you don't have a criminal record. Down the line, you have to have good grades so that the colleges that are looking at you in the ninth grade, they say this kid has some stuff going for him. And everything now from the ninth grade to the twelfth grade is being looked at.

The kids understand only that they want to be rich one day. But how do we get there? What does that process look like? Or they want to go to college. What's that process? I just found out that the core grades that these kids need goes back to the ninth grade. But their ninth grade year they're not mature enough to understand that. So they flunk or they get low grades their ninth grade year and then when they do get the maturity in the eleventh and twelfth, it's almost too late. And now all of their core grades are Fs and Ds, below average. I tell them, this is gospel here, this is the truth: You need to start off on a fast start and get your core grades to a point where colleges notice you.

In my classes, we're making a lot of headway. Kids came in rough and rugged and don't want to listen, but we came up with a system together. We built the foundation for our class and now things have been so productive because they understand my system. The kids at the beginning of the year didn't understand my system. My system basically is for us to understand each other. What are my goals? My goals are to teach you the health and P.E. that I need to teach you in order for you to get a successful grade. Your goals are to grasp whatever I'm teaching you, process it, and then utilize it to make yourself a better person.

That's why my job as athletic director is so critical because I can hold kids accountable. Once you tell me you want to be a student athlete, I've got something to hold you accountable. If you want to participate in sports, you gotta stay in the classroom and excel. I don't want just average. I don't want kids coming up to me when it's time to play and say, "Coach, am I eligible?" I want you to already know that. I want you to go into that class knowing you need either an A or a B. I don't want to accept average. I don't want to accept mediocrity. That's not what we're about. Because when you go into that big world out there, it's about competing. You gotta compete for jobs, you gotta compete for scholarships, you gotta compete for everything, income. So what I want them to understand and realize that it's a good competition, but you gotta prepare yourself early so that when you do get to college, you don't get put on the bench because you're ineligible or because you don't have the skill set.

We're gonna work on your skill set, your fundamentals and your academic progress so that when you do get out there, you get all aspects of life. When I was a competitor, first one to eat, first one to finish, first one to get a good grade, I wanted that girl, it was everything. Me and my boys competed at everything. So if I wasn't competing, I was probably asleep. But that's just the values that my dad and my mom put in me—that you need to be the best student athlete out there so that your blessings will come down upon you in so many ways that you make the choice, not somebody else making choices for you.

My student athletes are now doing progress reports. I want my coaches to hold the kids accountable for their grades, so that they're always academically eligible to play. Then first semester we get eligible before second semester again. If the kids don't get a 2.0 second semester, they can't play football first semester next year. So we gotta hold them accountable so that all the grades will be above 2.0 or more right now so that next year they can play.

The mindset changes by doing it that way. I don't want kids coming here asking me, "Hey, can you check my GPA?" No! If you got three As and a B, you know you're eligible, you don't have to ask me no questions. If you got two As and two Cs, you don't need to ask me no questions. If you got two Fs and two Ds, yeah, you better come back. Then the next semester you just go in there playing. You don't have to worry about your grades; you just continue with the standards and the practices that got you those As and Bs last semester.

All my kids sit up front. All the distractions are in the back. The teacher should know you; they should have a relationship with you by the second, third day of classes. How do you do that? Go talk to them. Say, "I wanna get an A in your class. I wanna develop a relationship with you so that if I start sliding, you not only tell me, but you tell my coaches and my parents." I want them to do that. Learn to be proactive. That will benefit you all your life.

Athletics is a guideline for life. You go out there and compete every day. You wanna write the best book. I wanna be the best A.D. She wants to be the best principal. He wants to be the best basketball player. You compete every day. You want to be the best father for your children. And those things are valuable because sports puts those values in you. I don't go out

on the athletic field thinking I just want to tie today. I'm gonna let my op-
ponent get me down and I'm gonna lose. I just wanna build his character.
What? Nobody does that. I wanna go out there to win. So when you do
those things, that will help your foundation grow.

Every choice that you make can dictate your future, so where do you want
your future to go? I wanted my kids to be successful. I got a beautiful wife,
I got four beautiful kids, I've traveled the world. Did I make it to the NBA?
No, but I was close. Did I live in Italy, did I live in Israel? Yes. Who can
say that? Did I win a state championship in football? Yes. I've lived my life.
I want people to live theirs. I want my kids to be more successful than me.
Why are you here? God has a purpose for everything. I know I'm supposed
to be here. I know that every day in my life, coming here will embrace the
process in front of me.

I feel like I am meant to be at West Charlotte. It happened because the
head basketball coach was about to leave and I interviewed for the job. I
thought it was a great interview, that might have me selected. But it was given
to Jacoby, a BMT here who's a great guy who has a relationship with the kids.
Still, I was devastated. Lord, I thought that was me. But at the end of the
interview, the principal said, "Coach Ivory, I think something's gonna open up
to where we're gonna meet again." I didn't know what that meant.

"Well, if you need anything, let me know," I said. I even called Jacoby and
told him, "Congratulations. If you need a JV coach, take a look. I just want
to be involved. It's my dad's alma mater."

I went and interviewed at Hopewell High, but didn't get that one. That
hurt, because I had a good resume. And then, all of a sudden the A.D. here
left and they called me back and said, "Titus, would you mind putting in for
the A.D. position?"

I didn't have any A.D. experience, but I'd had a whole lifetime of sports and I had a background in sports management and kinesiology.

"Yeah, I would love to," I said.

I applied for the job and got it.

And that's when people started saying, "I'm gonna pray for you every day." But it was Him putting this into my path. Working at my dad's school, working at my aunt's school, working at my grandmother's school, and graduating from here, I think, back in '38 or something like that. It brought tears to my eyes when I got the job. Putting the West Charlotte gear on, it didn't feel right at first, all my boys saying, "You're a traitor, man!" When we play North Meck, I wear my little lanyard because I want them to know where I came from, but I want them to also know what I'm representing now.

* * * * * *

My first day this semester, I called three parents during class because I just couldn't get their child to respect what we were trying to do. And I had three supportive parents but it takes a caring teacher to do just that. During class, I had to call the parents and say, "Hey, your momma wants to talk to you." And each student in the class was like, "Yeah, Momma." That's the thing that I want to do is bring parents back into their kids' lives every day. I will call you every day if I have to so that I get your son doing the right things.

But when you do call a parent and the kid comes back with a nonchalant attitude like nothing changed, that's disappointing. There was a kid that cussed me out because I took his basketball. He was in there shooting and he wasn't supposed to be. I said, "Put your ball away." He didn't want to put it away. I told him three times and he didn't put it away, so I took his ball. He said, "You're gonna give me my f---ing ball."

I called his momma and said, "Ma'am, I got your son's ball but I told him to put it away three times, and he had words for me. He cussed me out." Mom said, "Listen, you keep that ball." Because I was prepared to give it back to him the next day. "You keep it. He just donated that ball. Wait 'til he comes home." And that was my dad, that was my mom, right there. And I was like, "Thank you, but I don't get this often. I don't get supportive parents like you."

That was huge for me. Now, with that kid, every day we talk. He came the next day and apologized. "Coach, I'm sorry." That first week we weren't best friends but now, we dabbing each other up. I still got his ball right over there—his momma told me not to give it to him. Because she said not to give it back to him. He's a great kid, gonna run track for me. But that day he chewed me out. He actually stood in front of my door and wouldn't let me come in my own office. I was like, man, get out of the way. He was just overreacting to a situation. It's situations like this where we have good kids, but they get caught in a situation in the community, and when they get caught, they don't have the foundation behind them to pull 'em back. But out there, they just got the friends that want to enhance the situation, throw flame on it.

I told another kid, "I need you to run track for me." He asked one of his friends, "Hey, should I go run track?" The friend said, "No, come home with me and play videogames all day." I said, "That's not the advice you need." That's the mindset, but that's not the advice you need. Because this kid is one of the fastest things I've ever seen, but can't get him out of this mindset that he wants to go home and play Madden every day. But if he came to run track, he could potentially earn a scholarship, easily.

With this kid, I'm competing against a videogame, his friends and then possibly a parent that doesn't push him. So you got three things up against you. I tried to get him to run indoor. He said, "I'm not gonna come out. I ain't gonna do it." So I said, "You gonna do outdoor?" and he said, "Yeah, I'll do outdoor." Then he asked his friends and they said, "Nah, you should come play videogames with me."

You're just competing against so many different things out there that you can't get through to that kid. But I'm gonna keep doing it until he gets out there. He's in the ninth grade. I told him, if you do this now, when you become a senior, you can be the fastest dude in the state. He's that fast. But I'm not going to give up. I don't give up on anybody. I will keep pushing you. He's a good kid, and he knows he's fast. People always tell me I'm doing too much. I told my wife and she said, "They're not doing enough." And now anytime anybody says that to me, I just say, "You're not doing enough." I hit 'em over the head with that. The kids tell me, "Coach Ivory, you're doing too much, stay off my back." Then I tell them, "You're not doing enough. Try to figure out what enough is so that success will be easier for you. Every choice that you make out here is going to determine your future."

When I was young, my friends had respect for who my parents were. My parents opened their house to a lot of people. I actually never went to parties outside of my house because my parents always let me have them. Kids used to spend the night at my house. We never really went to spend a night at other people's houses because they opened our house up to everybody else. I remember having forty kids at my house one day. But that type of family atmosphere just allowed me to be that kid that had the cool parents. Were they strong in foundation and discipline? Yes. But they were people I could confide in, who I could tell the truth to, who loved me up and down and gave me whatever I needed to become successful. But all my friends respected them. I don't see that a lot these days.

TEN MEN

* * * * * *

I'm trying to change a culture. I don't like to talk about people who preceded me, but this community hasn't joined together in certain aspects in a few years. I've had coaches that were upset with me. I've had cheerleaders, you'd be amazed who I've come down on. They say, "Mr. Ivory, you're doing too much." "Well, you got to do a little bit better. You're not doing enough." I've had kids out here picking up trash for not having their pants up that day. "I got green sticks back there, come to my office, pick up some green sticks and you're gonna do some work, because your appearance isn't professional, so that tomorrow when I see you, you look professional. This is a punishment for how you let yourself go a little bit." Every choice that we make builds our character.

Not long ago, I had a conversation about that in my class and I said, "Listen, if you do something that is out of the ordinary but it's a positive thing, it could probably go viral in seconds." But our mindset tells us, nah, I wanna fit in. Sometimes they believe doin' the wrong thing is right. Or getting good grades—doing the right thing—is the wrong thing to do. Like if I go out there and get all As, I'm not going to promote myself, I'm gonna keep that a secret. Why would you have that mentality? Because it's not the norm? Don't do that to yourself. Promote the fact that you go home and study. Or promote the fact that you wanna go home and read a book. Promote the fact that you don't want to fight, you just want to stay out of trouble and do the right things. Doing the right things nowadays is pretty much corny.

As adults we need to expect more, demand more from our kids. In a lot of cases, our low expectations come out when the child gets suspended or when they get their grades or their report cards. "What happened to my son?" I have a lot of good support over here, I do. Now, in any corporation you're gonna have one or two that have nonchalant attitudes that just don't buy in the same way you buy in. When I first got here, a lot of people said, "We got a special kid over here and you gotta understand what West Charlotte represents now." But I said, "No, stop stereotyping these kids. Yeah, we got a special kid, but it's OK to pull your pants up. It's OK not to use profanity in front of adults."

I don't do mediocre. I don't do that at all. If you're gonna put on a jersey that says West Charlotte, you're gonna put it on with pride and have the utmost respect for that. If you don't wanna do that, then I'll hook you up with the rec center or the church, but if you're gonna put that on, then you're gonna put that on with pride.

My dad was the first black to play in the Shrine Bowl—him and Johnny Love. So if he did that and went through that period and wore his jersey to make this school a better place, then we're gonna respect that. Mo Collins who just passed away two years ago was a great coach. He had this thing turning around in the right direction and he had the same mindset that I do. Nobody's on varsity until that day your name's on that list. If your name ain't on that list, you're not on varsity that week. That's my mentality. Every week. So if you don't step up to the plate and represent West Charlotte for who it is and for who you are, then you're not gonna participate—that's the bottom line.

People ask me, "Why do you go over there with such an uplifting attitude?" I love changing people to make them better student athletes. We have conversations every day. I try to uplift them in so many ways. A lot of times, people just don't understand where these kids are coming from. When I worked with the police department, you got kids because they got arrested. Well, now these are kids that I'm trying to keep out of that situation.

But this place, in the last three to four months, I've seen great improvement in some of the attitudes of my athletes, some of the understanding that it is becoming a new culture. I have some great coaches. I've got a great faculty up there doing a great job from the academic standpoint. West Charlotte is going to change, but I want it to change for the better, not continue to do what we've been doing in years past. It's about changing the culture every day, day in and day out.

It's hard not to be excited. We're working on using the swimming pool for the whole community. Bringing in Park & Rec, Friendship Baptist, McCrorey Y, partnering together and using the whole community to embrace the blessing that we have down here in this new football field. We're gonna do camps, enrichment, field trips—we're gonna do a lot of powerful things community-wide. The rec center here in West Charlotte that just got renovated, people have come up to me talking about bringing national football, flag football leagues to the campus. They come up to me talking about bringing free football camps to the campus. Then we're gonna do a lot of tutoring, enrichment, and mentoring. We're really broadening the community. We want people to start seeing West Charlotte as a viable, educated community again. It's always been here, but now we're going to see it again. I want our kids to come back when they are twenty-five or twenty-six and say, "Coach, I appreciate what you did for me at the school. I appreciate how you held me accountable for what I was doing and I thank you."

JERRY McJUNKINS

A proud native of Charlotte's West Side, Jerry McJunkins has been a fixture of the North Carolina arts scene for more than four decades. McJunkins, who specializes in pastel, oil paint, and charcoal portraits, has received acclaim in the studio as well as the courtroom, where he has covered such high-profile cases as Jim Bakker, Susan Smith, Henry Louis Wallace, and Josh Griffin. Diagnosed late in life with dyslexia, McJunkins has overcome many hurdles en route to success. He began drawing as a young child and honed his skills through Central Piedmont Community College, but his most valuable experiences were gained as a portrait sketch artist at Carowinds amusement park, which solidly prepared him for courtroom sketch art. Jerry, who works primarily as a portrait artist at Dillard's SouthPark, also teaches group seminars and maintains an active studio in the Plaza Midwood neighborhood where he teaches drawing to students.

TEN MEN

I n the '50s, my family moved to University Park. I went to West Charlotte, graduated in 1968. Went to Northwest for middle school. Now they focus on the arts, but when I went to Northwest it was just survival of the fittest.

I have an older brother and two younger sisters. I was raised by a stepfather. That was a challenge. My parents owned a business at Five Points, right behind the Mechanics & Farmers Bank. It was called the Golden Bull. My mom owns that building there, that strip of buildings. Their store was like a soda shop; it was once a drugstore. When they went in, it had a grill and booths for the kids to eat hamburgers and hot dogs. My mom was famous for her hamburgers because she made them fresh.

It was named after the university's mascot, because back then the place was somewhat safe, there weren't any issues, really, so kids went all over that neighborhood. It was very busy. There was a pool room right beside it. So you have the barber shop where it is today, still the traditional barbershop that was on the corner, Golden Bull, kids' hangout, a pool room, and a laundromat. You could wash your clothes, play pool, go eat, and get your haircut.

* * * * * *

I didn't notice my artistic ability until after high school. The reason I focused on physical things was because I had a reading handicap. I didn't know what was wrong. I didn't understand why I could not read. Instead of actually reading words, I was remembering them.

In 1975 I started taking a night class, trying to improve my reading. A lady who was teaching at night school recognized my handicap. She said, "You know, Jerry, you're dyslexic!" My response was that I didn't know I looked like that. And once she explained it, my life flashed before me.

If I look at sixty-nine, right off, it's ninety-six. If I'm making a sandwich and I'm not thinking and I get jelly out of the refrigerator, peanut butter out of the cabinet. The next day when I go look for the jelly, what's in the refrigerator? The peanut butter. If you don't focus, you can reverse things. Dyslexia might work for me in the arts. Some things that I do, I reverse.

But I have good comprehension. Comprehension is a positive thing for dyslexia, because I needed to remember, even though I didn't understand why. That teacher recognized that, she saw it. And I see it too in kids—if I put something before them and ask them what it is. If they say sixty-nine when it's ninety-six, then they have it.

* * * * * *

My mom is good at business and has a nice sense for design. She likes to arrange, so most likely my gift came from her. My stepdad was a very simple man. I think he died in '72. We weren't close—I just reminded him that my mom had somebody else in her life. I never met my real dad. He was from Fayetteville. If I ever saw him, I don't remember. My stepfather, though, was influential in a positive way as far as my learning business. Even though he couldn't read, he was a hustler, he was an entrepreneur. He had a business in Brooklyn, which is now called Second Ward. He had a business there, another one in Greenville, like a café, and Graham Street.

The businesses were primarily café, jukebox, hot dogs, hamburgers, beer, cigarettes. My mother was the brains and he was the brawn. Primarily, he was just on his own. He also had a knack for buying and selling cars. He'd go to the rural part of North Carolina and might buy a '57 Chevrolet for $300 or $400 and bring it back and sell it for $700 or $800. So he was always making money.

TEN MEN

He and my mother had a good relationship and were together until his death. My two younger sisters were his kids. She was married once to my older brother's father, and then I was in between the first and second marriage. I was in the middle. I didn't understand what that really meant at the time; it didn't shape me.

Me and my brother were pretty tight, we just always supported each other. I looked up to my brother and I felt that he could do no wrong! But I can honestly say that the business part of my stepfather strongly influenced us … being independent, strong, powerful. Guys would come in the pool room, and they knew it was Star's place they couldn't mess around. For example, you could not come into his pool room with your shirttail out and no shoes. That was his name, Star. Alexander Star. But the one thing I can say is that in the last few years of my life, I have had a father figure that has adopted me as his son. His name is Joseph C. Howard.

* * * * * *

Charlotte was very segregated but as kids that didn't bother us. In our own world, we enjoyed each other. We didn't care about white boys—they had their thing, we had ours. Girls, parties. I never really hung out with a bunch of guys. I didn't need a group to hang with to be who I am. Peer pressure did not affect me. In high school I just had one close friend, Alan Neal, and we'd do things together. If I did anything wrong, I did it by myself. All the teachers were black. You usually didn't even like the teachers because they were hard on us, man. Having dyslexia, not knowing what it was and thinking that the teachers didn't like me … a lot of times I kinda cut up trying to make people laugh and stuff, making jokes. Especially at that time too, they'd say, won't your father come to class or come to lunch and I knew there ain't no way that's gonna happen. I didn't even dream about asking him to do that. They were kind of depressing times. Back then, I thought I might become a scientist. I always wanted to know how things work—that's always been my curiosity. I remember as a kid in third grade, there was a barber who'd say, "Jerry, what you wanna be?" I said, "I wanna be a scientist when I grow up." Had to be eight. I wanted to know how things work. Went into my mom's TV to see how it worked, almost got electrocuted. Took apart a gun, just to see how it worked. Now I know how things work. I understand. Emotionally, as a courtroom artist, I understand what it takes to capture someone visually—when people are trying to hide something or fear, hurt, anguish. So you try to illustrate that in a drawing.

* * * * * *

In 1969, I was accepted into a government program where you could get a check to go to a community college, to buy supplies and get an education. They showed us how to pursue a job and we got a grant for a community college and I chose advertisement. Under the umbrella of advertisement, you have design, illustration, and graphics. So you take the commercial art course and you take all areas and find out where your strength lies. Then that's the one you focus on in the second and third quarter. Illustration was my focus because I knew in the other two main courses you had to read, even though I would have liked to take design or graphics. So I had to go with the less academic course. I started in 1969, lasted a year and a half. During that time, getting a check, still getting high, that's what was happening at the time in '69, drugs, make love not war. I had a friend who knew somebody in organized crime. I was playing music with different groups in the club scene, and the friend said, "Hey, they will buy us the trucks, truck equipment and everything, and they will fund us if we play for them for the club they're building in Florida. We would be the house band. We'll pay 'em back."

House band for a Florida club to launder the money, the drug money. I was the liaison between the drug guy and the group, the band. I would communicate what they wanted from us—just to perform and put the money in there and do what they ask us to do. It was legit; we had an agent booking us gigs because we were good musicians. We had a group called Fungus Blues. Central Florida was the drug connection to Charlotte. There was a lady who was the main drug dealer there. They bought land to build a club in a town there, which they started to build, but it was held up because they were under investigation at that time. The feds were closing in. The handwriting was on the wall. They put me up in an apartment. I stayed there and grew my own marijuana on the property.

One day being high in town, I stole a bicycle. I was thinking nobody knew me, which was stupid. Everyone knew me. It was a small place. I took a bicycle from a display in front of a hardware store, just got on it and rode off. Don't you think everybody in town saw me ride? That turned out to be a good thing. Know why it was good? Here in Charlotte, my parents were in business, if I ever get in trouble, they always get me out. This time I couldn't get out. Couldn't get out of jail. So I laid there and said—and this is where my science came in—I said either I need to make some changes or this is going to be my life.

When I got out, I started looking at what this life is all about; I needed to do something. I came back to Charlotte, got my old apartment back off of Rozzelles Ferry Road and I started working for my mom. I knew I needed to do something, and that's when Jehovah's Witnesses knocked on my door, in 1974. So I started getting my life back in control and stop wasting talent.

I went back to Central Piedmont. Also I went to night school because I wanted to improve my reading. Witnesses do a lot of reading.

During that 1969 to 1973 or `74 around that time, I'd be sketching, drawing people. I drew a few girls, hey, I had something going there. After getting out of jail, coming back here, I said let me pick up where I left off in '69. But this time I had to pay for the program, of course. So I went back and I finished. This time after finishing, I learned some basic principles: what sells, why it sells, who's interested in what particular art. I put in an application at an advertisement place, almost got the job but I couldn't fill out the application. I had everything. They must have realized that I could not spell so they tried everything in their power to be nice to me. And I wasn't honest enough to say I just can't do it well.

Then I got a job at Carowinds, a sketching internship. A caricature artist said, "I can teach you." That's when they had charcoal drawings and they were supplying the pastel and paper. They supplied everything; it was excellent training and development of one's talent! Out of $5, you made $1.35 off each drawing. They get the rest. So to make any money you almost have to do like thirty drawings. On a Saturday you could do fifty drawings; you drew fifty people as fast as you could. I did that for nine summers. It was good. Excellent practice. I saw that, it was the science. I saw that from when I began at the end of the year, next year was getting better and better and faster and faster. That took me to the mall. First I went to a frame shop. It was just a little gallery where they did frames; they had paintings and stuff. In Charlottetowne Mall, the first mall for Charlotte, which then became Midtown Square. Before I got to that point, after Central Piedmont, I did any kind of work, and my wife was a graphic artist. She did more supporting me than I supported her. I mean she supported me not only financially and as an artist too; she was behind me. We would do some jobs together—special event jobs as sketch artists.

TEN MEN

Dillard's at SouthPark helped my career tremendously. When I left Midtown Square, I went to Dillard's. And they allowed me to be an artist in residence. This was like twenty years ago. I was inside that store by the shoe department. We had a symbiotic relationship. They literally helped me with my career. They're good people. They even helped me sell my stuff.

I have had my challenges! There was a district manager, who at one point came down and told the store manager that he didn't want me there. So I approached the district manager and asked him, "Why don't you want me there?" He said, "Jerry, you got good work, I like your work, but when I'm walking into the store, the first thing I don't want to see is you." His face started getting red. He called another person that was empathetic because he thought maybe I was gonna flip on him or something. He said, "Only place your stuff can be is in customer service. You can be there, nowhere else." I would've been tucked away up on the third floor. So I left some samples in customer service and got together with some guys from Iran who were selling paintings in a gallery in the mall. So they let me set up in the store window doing portraits. Less than a year later, a nice lady from Dillard's said, "Hey, Jerry, they told that district manager to leave. They fired him." So I went to Dillard's to the same store manager and said, "Hey, Jim, where can I set up?" He said, "Right where you were before." Apparently, the district manager had some issues that probably cropped up in another place. Dillard's, as well as the SouthPark management, it's a good place. I'm still there, twenty years or so, at SouthPark. Sometimes, as an artist it can be frustrating. Like the Arts & Science Council use artists for fundraising in the beginning of the year. I don't work for them like I used to, but they'll have me go out, sitting there during a special event. They'll send me to Belk or Wachovia, whatever, and say this is where your money's going to, people like me. That's a lie. It was going to me right then, but after the gig is over, I don't get a job for the rest of the year; other prominent artists do. As a matter of fact, I challenged them. Maybe that's why they don't call me.

One time I was working at some club, wining and dining these people. I think it was Wachovia, some big corporation, so he came in with two secretaries and pitched how great the arts and science are. "When you go to a city and you see artists like this, that brings culture to the city," he says. "Like this artist here," pointing right at me. They all clap and their little entourage starts walking out. "I really appreciate what you said there," I commended him, "but I want to work more than just this time of year." He said, "Do you have an application?" I said, "Yeah, but you don't call me." He said, "Well, put your name on, blah, blah, blah," and they left. So that was it. One of the Belks, we did a fundraiser for them. They had us there at the corporate office for lunchtime. The people come down and get a free sketch and then the Belk— it's always interesting too, around February—one of the Belk brothers, he came down and says, "That's very nice, you're a nice artist," he said. "Do you know this is Black History Month?" Asked me that, did I know that? I said, "Yeah, but I like to be black the other eleven months too." One time, I did this huge forty-eight-by-thirty-six-inch illustration of a piano and music composer, Loonis McGlohon, who worked often for the Arts and Science Council. I dropped it off at the office to see if anyone was interested in purchasing it. Three weeks later, I received a phone call and was told that someone threw it away. I was devastated! So it's out there some-where even though they settled with me for a third of what it was worth.

My career as a courtroom artist began in 1986 or '87, during the PTL scandal. One of the Channel 6 news producers apparently heard about me as a sketch artist and they called me and said, "Hey, do you think you can do sketches for us in court?" I said, "Sure." The application was, bring a pad, sit at the producer's desk, and sketch that guy over there, across the room. I did. He said, "We'll pick you up in the morning." And that did it, that started my career as a courtroom artist. I'm still doing it. I was there for Johnny Cochran defending heavyweight champion Riddick Bowe, for the trial of General Petraeus, and the court-marshalling at Fort Bragg of Sergeant Bergdahl. I don't do it as often as I used to, but I was at the Dylann Roof trial and the mayor, Patrick Cannon's trial. There was a strangulation of a black man here in Charlotte a few years ago. Lawrence Davis was the attorney representing the black guy. Police used to be able to put a chokehold on people. They stopped that practice. So they had a chokehold on him and he died as a result of that chokehold. He had the case, ironclad case. We came out of high school together, West Charlotte. He got a court order and a key to the jail. I went to the jail, telling jailers what to open, I want that, move that out of the way. Imagine that, I had authority that day! In getting ready for opening arguments, they need to see the floorplan, so I did the graphics and they put up a board in court. So I did the graphics of where they brought him in that night to book him for the charge and where they walked him back and where they found him dead. The thing was, the same jail this guy died was one of the jail cells that I had been locked in during my youth, for possession of hashish. The same cell. Before I turned my life around.

* * * * * *

Charlotte is a very conservative city. If I was a white man, my financial state would be completely different. Here's a case in point. I did a nice, conservative, cute little girl, maybe three years old, Country Day-like, out in the backyard, flowers, beautiful, and it was on display. One morning I was coming in, and that's when I was inside the store. Inside the store they have a number of mirrors. You can look at one mirror and see over here, you don't have to be looking at the person. I came up to my display. I saw three little girls that looked like the girl I was working on with their mothers. Three of them, looked just like the little girl that I was just finishing up. They saw me and I'm lookin' at them. They looked at each other. It was like the sheriff that came in on "Blazing Saddles"—they just packed up and left. Prejudice. I was a black man. They most likely thought it was a white person who did the portrait. Sometimes I'll get questions. They ask me, "Did you really do that?" Did I use a machine? I have no problem. It's their problem. I'm good. I have many other white clients who have supported my art and didn't see race as an issue, and I'm thankful for that. A case in point—a few years ago, the federal government here in Charlotte asked if I would bring the court art from the past twenty years or more of high-profile federal court cases. Today, here in Charlotte, on Trade Street, I have had the privilege and the honor of having several pieces hanging throughout the courthouse, in the jury room and offices. It's like my own personal gallery. Some of the pieces are throughout North Carolina federal courthouses. And I think all the people who are not there to see my race, but my talent as an artist.

* * * * * *

I met my wife at CPCC. I was making this transitional change in my life. I saw her and she was taking a photography class and the same courses I was at the time. I was playing music too, with Fungus Blues Band and a jazz group, Spectrum. l would see that same woman at some of the places I would play. I said, "Before I straighten up, settle down, I'm gonna mess around one more time." And that's what it was. That was it, the last time.

TEN MEN

Isn't that ironic? She's the woman that I said I messed around with, one more time. She was the woman who enjoyed jazz music. We both enjoyed art when I met her, taking the same course at CPCC. I introduced her to what I was doing and she became one of the Jehovah's Witnesses.

We got married and had two beautiful daughters. She was a graphic designer at the *Observer*. After the job was outsourced to another country, she said she wanted to get something that they can't outsource. She's been a nurse for almost four years now, working just two nights a week. Good job. Works on the baby floor; she loves that. We have two beautiful daughters who were my whole world. When they were young they were with us all the time! As a matter of fact, my daughters were never in a daycare. They were with us when they were growing up. I would take them to court to do my cases and they would draw the criminals too.

My youngest daughter was recently in *Vogue* magazine. She's a vocalist and plays the cello and models too. She just did a campaign with Kenzo, and she has an album out on the Columbia label. That daughter is in Los Angeles; her artistic name is Kelsey Lu McJunkins. My other daughter is a violinist in New York, living in Brooklyn. She's a regular with The Roots on "The Tonight Show with Jimmy Fallon," plays with Beyonce, and is different because she also plays a lot of classical music. Last month, she was soloist with an orchestra in New York. Her name is Jessica McJunkins.

They were with us everywhere we went. One thing that influenced them is we're Jehovah's Witnesses. That lifestyle influenced their behavior. Every-where we go people always said, "They're so nice and respectful." We taught them respect for people, basically, Bible principles. One could say, the Bible is the art to living! I have been truly blessed by the gift I have, but most importantly, I've had the privilege to share that gift in serving God and my fellow man.

ALVIN AUSTIN

Long before Alvin "Al" Austin was elected in 2013 to serve District 2 on Charlotte's City Council, he was highly regarded throughout the community as a dedicated public servant. A native Charlottean and graduate of University of North Carolina at Chapel Hill, Austin is known as among the city's most thoughtful and steady advocates for the Northwest Corridor. Among his key efforts is growing the area's tax base by identifying and repurposing buildings in older neighborhoods to attract new businesses and job opportunities for residents, pushing for a Northwest Corridor streetcar economic development, and for improved infrastructure such as streets and sidewalks, better code enforcement, and attracting grocery retailers to eradicate food deserts in the community. Along with Charlotte City Council, Austin, a member of the Kappa Alpha Psi fraternity, also serves as the Major Gift Officer for Johnson C. Smith University.

TEN MEN

W hen I was born in the 1960s, my family lived in one of the shotgun houses on Hill Street, which was in the Third Ward neighborhood in what is known as Uptown Charlotte today. My family moved to Cummings Avenue off of Beatties Ford Road, so the Northwest Corridor is my stomping ground. I grew up in the heart of the Northwest Corridor, went to school at the University of North Carolina at Chapel Hill and eventually returned home to West Charlotte where I stayed with my grandparents for a while. Back in 1988, I bought a condo on Cedar Street and my grandma said, "You just moved to where you were born." At the time, I wasn't making the connection; I just knew I liked the area. As the seasons have passed, I now understand what my grandma was saying. This community of family, neighbors, elders, peers—is where it all began for me. That's why it meant so much to me to try to do something for my community by serving in my various roles over the decades, including heading the historic McCrorey Family YMCA, raising dollars for Charlotte's only HBCU, Johnson C. Smith University, and serving as the Charlotte City Councilman for District Two.

I firmly believe the people in the Northwest Corridor have power but they must own it. Often, I feel like the community is looking for government to wave its hand and the whole world is right. But if we just turn that mirror around, we'd realize that we can transform our communities ourselves by investing in our neighborhoods through supporting each other, keeping our neighborhoods clean and safe, fighting for city, county, and state services, and advocating for home-grown businesses.

We can't rely on government to shape our world and our lives. So I continuously seek ways to empower community leaders and activists in our community's transformation. It's important for me to help all understand exactly what I can and can't do as a Charlotte City Council member in contrast to my colleagues on the Mecklenburg County Commission and the school board, as well as in contrast to elected officials at the state and federal government levels. There's so much power in our community once community members better understand what each elected body of government can and cannot do. Then we are better equipped to do it for ourselves.

From my perspective, change in our communities is a shared partnership, and I am proud to serve as partner and "wingman" within my role as a City Councilman. Early on in my first term, I developed a strategic plan for the Northwest Corridor in collaboration with presidents of the neighborhoods. This plan looked at challenges and opportunities of the neighborhoods along Beatties Ford Road to begin to transform and to empower the people. My district includes 120,000 residents bordered by the Uptown business district, including the BB&T Stadium and Bank of America Stadium, north to Northlake Mall, west where Walmart is located on Highway 16, and east to the University City YMCA. These communities have different goals, visions, and needs with residents who have different perspectives and biases; however, I am honored to partner with them to address issues and help their visions become realities.

For instance, we talk a lot about gentrification in our neighborhoods such as Cherry, Wilmore, Biddleville, and so on. But what happens oftentimes in our neighborhoods around Charlotte is that we have homeowners who may have allowed their houses to go into disrepair or get into substandard conditions that then get reported to the city's code enforcement. Unfortunately, those houses may have to be demolished. There are entities that see these homes with an eye for future development and reach out to the homeowner and say, "Hey I'll give you X amount of dollars if you sell it to me." So the homeowners sell their property and these entities purchase the property, upgrade it, and then resell at a market rate above the level that previous homeowner ever thought of. Then the change in the neighborhood begins, and those who have lived there all their lives find themselves unable to stay due to the change in the market rate value of their property and in their property tax rates.

My informal solution seeks to respond to the issue of gentrification by engaging members of our community and building relationships of trust. Many times, I'll call community members that I know and say, "Hey, look, this property over here is in really bad shape. How about we go over and take a look at it?" We look to see if we can repair it or I will call the city's Neighborhood and Business Services and ask what programs can help these folks. This way, we can work together on keeping the property in the hands of the community members who have established this community and have deep roots planted within it. This is a more informal way to address gentrification, but we have the capacity to do it. It just takes conversation with one another. While I wholeheartedly support and invite new residents to become a part of the Northwest Corridor community because it is inherently valuable to the overall growth of this area, I am certain that we must manage this growth in a more thoughtful and inclusive way. We have a duty to develop in ways that protect those who for generations have belonged to and invested in this community.

What I'm celebrating right now is that we now have some younger people who are positioned to lead our communities. We have had some phenomenal and great community leaders who have fought the fight. They've been fighting for twenty or thirty years, and they've kept their communities going, but now they're beginning to pass the torch to others to move forward into the next twenty or thirty years. A good example is the Oaklawn Park neighborhood, near Russell Avenue and Jennings Street. William Hughes and his wife, Tiffany, have become very involved not only with the neighborhood, but also serving on various city boards and commissions. He is the new neighborhood president. He sees issues, and we will go after them together. For example, there's an access ramp off LaSalle Street that goes onto I-77. It gives you only approximately fifty feet to merge into oncoming traffic but cars are going seventy miles per hour. I told him, "I can help you on city streets, but this happens to be a state issue. I can back you." So William targeted the NCDOT, getting them to put some focused energy into it and I backed him, and now an improved longer ramp is going to be part of the I-77 toll lane improvements.

We also have a new leader of the Historic West End Neighborhood Association (HWENA). This organization is comprised of eighteen neighborhood presidents who meet on the second Saturday of each month to discuss issues, strategies, and the vision for the Northwest Corridor. Calvin McDougal is the new president and he's bringing a new perspective to the dialogue of the group. We must tap into new leadership and have a succession plan to perpetuate growth in our communities. With the advent of leadership like Hughes and McDougal, I am more of a "wingman" and that's how I like to see it happen. I join the presidents in their visions and provide a lift. It takes grassroots leadership to transform the community. All the work cannot happen from the top down.

The expansiveness of my council district allows me to address issues in other areas of the city and gain insight that might work for the Northwest Corridor. For example, Mountain Island Lake near the Walmart and Highway 16 is more of a suburban area. Community members were extremely concerned about growth, traffic, and economic development. I worked in partnership with them for two years to try to find projects that would be helpful for that area but would not overwhelm them. The community residents put together a development committee and they went to work. Prior to this, I attended a meeting of about two hundred very angry people who were very frustrated. To their credit, community members said, "Here's our issues, let's form some committees, focus our attention, and figure out how we can help this process." By the grace of God about a year and a half ago, I began to talk with some developers that were looking at the property right across from the Walmart. These developers wanted to put a major corporate headquarters, high-end townhouses, better restaurants, a movie theater, etc., and just so happens earlier this year Corning decided that they wanted to move from Hickory, N.C. to the Mountain Island Lake area. That provided community members with the type of development they were looking to have in their community. I do the same thing for the Northwest Corridor, but it's tougher. I talk with developers, ride them though the areas, and ask them to imagine what would they do in concert with neighborhood leaders.

All and all there's a lot of positive change happening in the Northwest Corridor. Houses are increasing in value, corporations are investing in the area, and the infrastructure is ever-evolving. There's the $20 million from the city's Community Neighborhood Investment Program that's designated for the Five Points area and there's another $20 million from the city invested in the Beatties Ford Road/Sunset area. I am hoping these will be transformative to help the community create economic development and community pride. The Knight Foundation funded an executive director for the Historic West End Initiative. The executive director works for Charlotte Center City Partners to provide a cohesive and collaborative approach to the city's investment in the Historic West End. There's the federal and city $150 million infrastructure investment in the city Lynx Gold Line from Novant Health to just past Johnson C. Smith University. We've got the North Carolina Bar Association located on Rozzelles Ferry Road. We have a huge new housing development by the Housing Partnership just off of Cindy Lane and Beatties Ford Road—it's going to be like the Brightwalk development along Statesville Road.

Bobby Drakeford, an African-American developer, is building a senior adult community. It's about ninety-eight units near the Kappa Alpha Psi Fraternity house on Beatties Ford Road. We're expanding and improving the road way in front of McCrorey Family YMCA up to Sunset Road with bike lanes and infrastructure. The Mecklenburg County Park and Recreation department just put in a new park behind Friendship Baptist Church in partnership with the church. Flashing traffic signals are currently at Lakeview and Reames roads but people are having trouble navigating the right of way, so we're going to put in a new roundabout. This has been an issue since I was a child; I am happy to be a catalyst to help make this change. My life has been and continues to be about service. I am a servant leader. I think I am just wired that way.

DARRYL GASTON

Darryl Gaston, a Charlotte native, is a passionate and results-oriented advocate behind the turnaround of the historic Druid Hills Neighborhood, his birth home to which he returned years ago with a dream to restore the area's long-forgotten pride and luster. By acquiring homes and creating affordable housing for needy residents, as well as organizing police watch and beautification committees, Darryl, pastor of Smallwood Presbyterian Church, has brought a whirlwind of positive change to a neighborhood once characterized by its decline. As president of the neighborhood association, Gaston has initiated numerous public-private partnerships that have resulted in the community becoming safer, cleaner, and more attractive for investment. In 2009, largely due to the work spearheaded by Gaston, Druid Hills was named Charlotte's Neighborhood of the Year.

TEN MEN

I was born in June of 1961. I lived here on Edison Street in Druid Hills. Really, this street predates the community of Druid Hills. Where we're sitting right now was called Edison Heights and on the deed to this property, that's what this subdivision is called, Edison Heights. But in later years, we became known as Druid Hills. I still have an organized neighborhood association that's called the Edison Street Block Association, as well as the Druid Hills Neighborhood Association, because I want to hold on to that history. But as a child, I grew up here, in a house. My brothers did not grow up in a home; my parents actually lived in an apartment for a very long time. I had three brothers: William, Bernard, and John. I'm the youngest. John was the oldest, he's deceased. William is the next brother, he is honorably retired from the United States Army, after thirty years or so. My brother Bernard is a graduate of Johnson C. Smith University and retired from the State of North Carolina Employment Security Commission. And then I'm the baby boy. There's an eight-year difference between Bernard and myself. My parents were not interested in having any more children after John, William, and Bernard. Bernard was the baby for eight years, and then pops out Darryl, who upset and bumped him from his baby spot.

Growing up on Edison Street, I remember that we didn't have to lock our doors or close our windows in the summertime. I remember that all of the neighbors were people that I actually knew by name and that has changed now, in 2016, 2017. I knew that I could be cared for and nurtured—I didn't have to worry about hurt, harm, or danger from my residents. I could sit with my friends in the middle of the street at night or during the day because we didn't have a lot of traffic. People didn't have a lot of cars initially, but as they were able to grow and households and incomes grew, people were able to buy cars. My parents and others during the early '60s were instrumental in growing what they called the Edison Street Neighborhood Block Association.

DARRYL GASTON

They formed that association because they had a lot of new homeowners who were black people who were blue-collar working people, some were college-educated professionals, so we had the gamut from pastors, teachers, maids, chauffeurs, butlers, sanitation workers, principals, a little bit of everything. With everyone being new homeowners, the Edison Street Block Association was formed so that they could collect money and dues so that if anyone fell on hardship, they could help them with their mortgages.

In the late '40s, the Edison Street neighborhood was an all-white street. These houses were built for the white G.I.s after World War II. And we had the Ford plant, which is located on the Woodward/Statesville Avenue corridor, which later changed to the missile plant where bombs were made for the military. Some of the residents on this street were actually part of making those bombs and those missiles. But after they experienced white flight, black people began to move into the neighborhood, work hard, buy their homes. We had one man in the neighborhood, Mr. Miller, his porch was bombed by whites. They say it was the Ku Klux Klan here in the Corridor but when that happened, some of the other black men in the neighborhood and some of the surrounding neighborhoods began to keep a twenty-four-hour watch with Mr. Miller. They actually sat on their front porch with shotguns to help protect his home, because white people didn't want black people to move here. And where I'm sitting now, my grandparents were the third owners of this property. The first owners were a white couple, the second owners were a white couple, and then the third owners of this property were black people. Blanche and Cornell Holman, who were my grandparents.

That's why this property is so important to me. This is home; I lived here from 1961 up until about 1989. I moved away, did not leave Charlotte, but in 1996, I moved back to this home, house, to take care of my mother who had a stroke and eventually had to have a mastectomy due to breast cancer and

TEN MEN

then an amputation of a leg due to diabetes. So home is a place where I enjoy and I meditate. The carriage house is a space that is filled with my history. Everything in the room is typically an emotional attachment for me because it was either my great-grandmother's, my grandmother's, my grandfather's, my mother's, my great-aunt's, my great-uncle's, or people like that. So there's a story. Every piece in the carriage house, every piece in the bungalow, which we came through, that was built in the '40s, every piece has a story.

This is where I have been enriched and empowered to go forth and I was always told by the community that whatever you do in terms of education, you don't do it for yourself, you do it for other people. And remember to always be not only nice to people, but be kind to people, and treat people the way you want to be treated. You may not ever remember what I've done for you, but you will remember how I've treated you, so that's how I've lived my life. I believe that I'm a servant leader, and servant leadership is love in action.

Being a child of the '60s and '70s, I experienced men who were clean in their person, men who demonstrated a work ethic, men who demonstrated to me that education is important, men who demonstrated to me how to treat women and how not to treat women. I experienced men who purchased multiple properties and became landlords themselves. I experienced men who became doctors, lawyers, aldermen in other cities. I experienced men who demonstrated to me what it meant to be a servant from the standpoint of view that if we get a hard snow, the men get together and cleaned off the sidewalks and steps of every house on this street. I saw men who would shovel out driveways; we didn't have paved driveways per se. Some houses have them now, but a lot of them did not back in the day, and I witnessed men who helped other people, families, shovel out driveways, clean off cars, put chains on cars in the snow. I think that was very interesting for me to see—chains actually used on tires to navigate. I witnessed men from this street, more specifically my father, John Lee Gaston Sr., who would get out, dig out of the snow and travel to Concord to take my great-aunt Bessie clothing and food or to retrieve her and her daughter from her cold house. I experienced men who were willing to take a risk to help other people and to be better.

I also experienced some men who were very instrumental in starting the first Presbyterian church in the Statesville Avenue corridor, my father being one of those men. The church that I grew up in, my home church, Statesville Avenue Presbyterian Church, which is really the foundation for my being a third-generation Presbyterian and embracing what it means to be black and Presbyterian. In the city of Charlotte, in the state of North Carolina, and for the year of 2015, I was elected moderator of the Presbytery of Charlotte as a lay pastor or elder called to special services. I believe that I was the first because in the Presbyterian church, we typically don't allow you in the pulpit without a college degree and a master's degree. And I didn't attend seminary. I didn't attend a university of higher learning. But I'm an example of how whatever God has in store for you, he has in store for you. I recognize the fact of how education can take you to a place where your character will not let you stay. But I'm a product of how my character has taken me to a place and my character allowed me to stay and to perform and to be. So as a non-college-educated individual with a two-year course study work in sermon writing, teaching, preaching, sacraments, and the overall polity of the Presbyterian Church USA, I now pastor a church. An inner-city urban church. We have about 115 members on the roll. We have fifty individuals at service any given Sunday. We do two Bible studies, one at 12:00 noon and one at 6:30 on Wednesday. We're actively engaged in the mission and the ministry of the Men's Shelter of Charlotte. We do some work with Urban Ministries. We also partner with an organization in the Loaves and Fishes pantry. So we do

TEN MEN

a vibrant ministry, we have a campus ministry where we work with Johnson C. Smith University, and we provide stress-care kits for the college students while they're taking exams. We're excited to be a part of that.

I grew up with the first black police officer in the city of Charlotte. His name was John Lyles. I also grew up here in this community with the first black female area superintendent, Kathleen Crosby. I also have the privilege of sitting under the feet of Dr. Jacquelyn Dunham Nelson, who is a graduate of Morgan State University. She grew up here on Edison Street, went away and lived in Washington D.C. for more than forty years where she was an educator, but she moved back. She's part of the fabric of the community again, having been a child here, now a senior citizen here. I also grew up in this area of Edison Street and Druid Hills with the first black female disc jockey. Her name is Hattie Leeper. But her handle is Chatty Hattie. Also in my family, there is a cousin-in-law who was married to one of my family members, she's Joanne Graham. She used to be "this is Joanne Graham from WGIV Charlotte North Carolina." Joanne is still alive today and has two children.

Of course, I can't talk about my community of Druid Hills without talking about those individuals who are experiencing homelessness because they, too, are my neighbors. That's kind of a tough place for me because whenever it gets extremely cold I'm concerned because there's a population who experience homelessness who have no desire to be homed, so they experience and suffer the pains of the elements and cold, extreme cold and wind and rain. So whenever it rains I'm a little concerned, even though I know we need rain. Whenever it's extremely cold I'm a little concerned because I know people who actually live outside.

There was a white man who lived in this area at the corner of Statesville Avenue and Woodward who was homeless and I watched him for like four years. I offered him coffee; he would take that. He would not take money;

he wouldn't take a sleeping bag. He was a person who I learned because I watched him on my morning walk. He would get up off of his wood pallet that was covered in cardboard, wipe off the cardboard that had dew or condensation on it. He would then fold it up. He would get the pallet, pick it up, and place it in between some trees and over brush and he would place the cardboard there. Then he would go into his pocket and take out his comb and comb his hair. He would put on his coat and straighten up his clothes and then off to Center City he would go for the day. And I saw him in Center City so that's why I knew that he would leave Druid Hills and go to Center City to spend the day where I can imagine that's where he got maybe some food or some beverage and whatever resources he was able to tap. Then in the evenings, he would come into the community, put out his bed, and live here. I once shared his story with Leadership Charlotte on the top floor of the Bank of America building and participants in that class were reduced to tears. I too became tearful in knowing that it's important for us to have eyes for people and that we need to be intentional about that regardless of our hue or skin color, regardless of our social or economic background. Because we're all visible, vital, and valuable.

* * * * * *

I've had people say to me, "Darryl, I'm so happy to see you back in Druid Hills taking your neighborhood back," and I say, "I never let my neighborhood go." I'm back here to build upon, to encourage, to create a base of neighborhood capacity. I do see that there is a shortage of grassroots activism and community advocacy. One thing I knew we needed was some type of economic development program. So I applied for a Neighborhood Matching Grant from the City of Charlotte in the amount of $25,000 because, along with some other partners and collaborative partnerships, we wanted to establish a leadership academy. We engaged Dr. Bryan Patterson from Johnson C. Smith University to serve as the dean of this leadership academy. Then we talked with Raymond Barnes in Druid Hills Academy, which is located right here and is the school I attended as a little boy. We asked Principal Barnes if he would handpick us fifteen or sixteen eighth-graders, not the top of the eighth-grade class but not the quote bottom-of-the-barrel of the eighth-grade class, but somewhere in between, who he felt would be good candidates for a leadership development program centered around core values, creating a base of working with residents. We had those eighth-graders committed on Saturdays to come. We had residents from the community who have lived here for forty, fifty, sixty years to go on different Saturdays to talk to these students.

This was a partnership with Druid Hills Academy, Charlotte-Mecklenburg Housing Partnership, City of Charlotte Neighborhood Services, Druid Hills Neighborhood Association, Johnson C. Smith University. They are student leaders, young neighborhood leaders. The program went on from like April, May, June, July, August. If I remember correctly, it was a five-month program and at the end of the program, we held a graduation ceremony for those students the first Tuesday of August of 2014. We presented them with presidential letters from President Barack Obama and hosted that event at our National Night Out, which is an initiative that we participate in every year in our neighborhood park, which is centered around crime and safety efforts and education. The children were very, very happy to receive those letters and to be acknowledged and highlighted. We won a $25,000 grant through the Druid Hills Neighborhood Association, a collaborative partnership with the Charlotte-Mecklenburg Police Department and the Charlotte-Mecklenburg Housing Partnership, we won a $25,000 grant from MetLife Insurance Company for our reduction of crime and disorder in the Druid Hills community. We also donated that $25,000 to Habitat for Humanity to build a house in the Druid Hills community.

Then we were afforded another opportunity though the Park and Recreation of Mecklenburg County. We entered a national grant competition for the national Park and Recreation. We had to submit a project that we would like to see happen here in the Statesville Avenue corridor, more specifically in Druid Hills. One day I got a letter that Druid Hills made it to the cut of twenty. So I was like, "Wow, we made it to the cut of twenty, good." So then I got another letter stating that we'd made it to the cut of ten, and then I said, "OK Lord, we're gonna win this grant." And it was for $25,000. Then I was notified by Lee Jones, Jim Garges, and James Williams of Park and Rec that Druid Hills had won that national grant for $25,000 for our project to create a community garden for our neighborhood of Druid Hills. So being the smart and intelligent person that I am, I took that $25,000 and used it as leverage and did a match with a Neighborhood Matching Grant. I applied for another $25,000, used the $25,000 from Park and Rec, which gave us $50,000 for our community garden.

The running joke in the city of Charlotte and Mecklenburg County is that Druid Hills has the most expensive community garden in the city and the county. I would offer that we do because it's a beautiful garden. We have concrete pavers and raised beds. We had the realtors from Mecklenburg County and Realtor Care Day to come in and do us some nice raised beds. We have a butterfly garden that is designed to attract pollinators so we can have the bees and butterflies, which are very important and pertinent to the growth of flowers and fruits and vegetables. We have this past fall, spring, and summer, we had greens, tomatoes, squash, radish, bell peppers, sweet potatoes, okra, figs, just a plethora of fruits that we were able to share with

TEN MEN

Second Harvest Food Bank. We were able to share with residents of the community. We were able to have children and young people to come into the garden and to educate them about where food actually comes from and to do away with that myth that our food and vegetables only come from the grocery store. Children now in the community have a heightened sense of awareness that "I can grow vegetables."

I can't help but go back to the fact of I matter. How do I know that I matter, why do I matter, and who do I matter to? And more importantly, what can I do to go out and help someone else know that they matter too? And that's why we do this work of community advocacy. Because we do matter. All people matter, regardless, good, bad, ugly, indifferent—we matter. And each person I believe that lives on this earth shares common values or core values. We all want to know that people see us, that we're important, that we're competent and that people care, that somebody cares for me, that someone cares for you. And it's not about always being in someone's face twenty-four hours a day, seven days a week. It's about connecting people and developing healthy, wholesome relationships. When we experience people who maybe do us wrong, whether they are elected officials, nonprofits, teachers, other professionals, whether they're neighborhood advocates or residents. When people show you their dark side, just say, "Thank you, Lord, for the blessing." Now you know that this person has revealed his or her true self to you.

I imagine Druid Hills transitioning to a place and space where people can live, work, and play, where the space and place is crime-free, a place and space that has adequate infrastructure, a place and space that is civic by design, that is intergenerational, that is inclusive of people of all backgrounds and skin colors, people of all sexual orientation, people who are educated and not so educated. I envision a place of variety of housing stock, from affordable to middle-class to high-end housing. I cringe sometimes at the fact of the word "gentrification" and I embrace the term "reinvestment."

This is what I know, that change comes slow but it comes. And I know that with us being located less than one-half mile from Uptown, Downtown or Center City, that our white brothers and sisters are coming back, the investors are buying up blocks here in Druid Hills, they're banking land and I see now how you cannot buy a house in this community for $25,000 or $30,000 anymore. You have to pay $50,000 and up. There are two properties that recently sold on Edison Street. One sold for $99,000 and the other sold for a little over $100,000. That has never taken place on this street, ever, but it's now taking place and it's happening. So I want to see my seasoned citizens be in a better place. If they do have to sell their properties, I want to see them be better off if they do. I personally am actively engaged in purchasing anything I can other than what I already own here on Edison Street. I'm not into flipping houses; I'm into purchasing foreclosed homes or taking houses that are beneath code level and bringing them up to code and making them affordable for people to have decent housing. I want people to know that there is hope.

THE WEST SIDE

By Tiffany Taylor

T*en Men* is intentionally focused on the plight of black males on Charlotte's West Side. Consequently, any fair assessment of their circumstances depends heavily on a demographic understanding of Mecklenburg County, which in 2015 rose to more than one million residents. The city of Charlotte, which accounts for some eighty percent of the county's overall population, is projected to grow by roughly fourteen percent through 2020. African Americans cumulatively make up about thirty-five percent of Charlotte's population. Some 157,000 black men reside in Charlotte, the largest population of black men in the state of North Carolina, according to the most recent U.S. Census data. Collectively, the largest proportion of black men reside in and around the Historic West End, thus serving as a bellwether for the city's social and economic vitality.

Charlotte's Historic West End encompasses several ZIP codes and includes neighborhoods where poverty and progress collide. This narrative is largely anchored within the greater West Side, which extends along Beatties Ford Road, a nexus for such issues as education, unemployment, incarceration, healthcare, etc. The Bureau of Labor Statistics reports that North Carolina's ten percent unemployment rate for African Americans exceeds the overall national unemployment percentage. In Charlotte alone, approximately 21,000 black men between the ages of eighteen to fifty-four are either unemployed or not a part of the city's labor force. Approximately 25,000 black men between the ages of eighteen to thirty-four are not enrolled in college or graduate school, compared to only 4,500 who are (American Community Survey ACS 2010). At face value, these numbers may seem small relative to the 157,000 black men that account for a major portion of the city's population. Consider, however, the impact such underemployment and relative lack of advanced education wields on the families and communities that are touched by the hands of these men.

Indeed, numerous studies have found that lack of education and high rates of unemployment have an impact not only on individual financial stability, but prove debilitating on one's well-being and mental health, particularly among African-American men. A recent study by Dr. Raj Chetty published through the National Bureau of Economic Research (2016) found that economic misfortune is likely to follow young children, boys in particular, throughout their lifespan. Moreover, young boys from low-income, high-crime communities work less over the course of their lives than young women and are more likely to resort to criminal activity rather than seek and obtain gainful employment. As a result, one can rightly assume the generational transference of these trends, portending negative future outcomes for predominately black communities where black men have been systemically abandoned by the public sector and are confined by their own societal misfortune.

Tiffany Taylor is the Research Associate for the Smith Institute for Applied Research at Johnson C. Smith University.

EPILOGUE

By Dr. Diane Bowles

While the situation for the vast majority of black men in the United States is dire, Johnson C. Smith University (JCSU) takes a strength-based view in *Ten Men: Examining the Passion and Progress of Black Men on Charlotte's Historic West Side.* Just as Ellison conjectures in *The Invisible Man,* "I am a man of substance, of flesh and bone, fiber and liquids ...", indeed the ten black men highlighted in this book are divergent thinkers made of substance, vision, tenacity, faith, conviction of character, commitment, and statesmanship. While reading these stories, we glean an intimate perspective of how these ten men navigate and internalize their environments, both immediate and global, and their realities against institutionalized and systemic barriers.

Ten Men is a seminal production of JCSU's Smith Institute for Applied Research, useful as a preliminary tool for examining the lives of black men within and affecting Charlotte's Northwest Corridor and Historic West End. We examined Charles Jones' determined faith that carried him through the fight for human rights. Jones operated in a faith that jail, segregation, nor the indecency of the Jim Crow South could not shake. A faith, matched with courage, loving family, and community supports, that transported him from a rock-throwing youngster to defending democracy in Vienna, Austria, to being a champion and pioneer in the fight for Civil Rights. Similarly, Colin Pinkney's tenacity propelled him from poverty and dysfunction to candor and grace by offering young black men a soft place to land inside his book club. Pinkney expanded their vernacular beyond generations of systemic destructive decay and possibly changed the trajectory of young men's lives by enforcing four simple rules: read, respect, reciprocate, and represent. Young professionals like Damian Johnson and Justin Harlow are shining examples of professionalism and strength-based modeling as they not only look to the Corridor as a place of hope but seek prosperity and quality of life, not just for themselves but for their neighbors and the generations after them. Divergent thinkers and educators like Dr. Melvin Herring and Titus Ivory who daily affirm the intrinsic value of our youth and positively impact the lives of the next black generations of leaders that will effect positive change within and throughout our immediate and global communities. Visionaries like Alvin Austin, Jerry McJunkins, Darryl Gaston, and Darrel Williams see beyond the tarnished and albeit brutish stereotypes and pour out their lives advocating and creating change. Moreover, as we examine and celebrate the lives of these mighty agents of change, we are reminded of our collective and historic value through their examples and stories highlighted in *The Corridor*.

Through this examination, we find recurring themes that include personal motivation, a broader world view through innovation and technology such as social media, reimagined masculinity, and perhaps most paramount is strong faith, community, and family supports. Furthermore, their stories illuminate how black male vitality and success need not be uncommon or absolute. Rather, their stories and successes highlight the importance of positive role models, afterschool programs, an expanded worldview, and networks of support so desperately needed in our community.

To foster the desperately needed change, the JCSU Smith Institute for Applied Research will further examine *how* to effect change within the Corridor by posing the research question, "How to use strength-based modeling and approaches to empower and ignite the young black men of Charlotte's Northwest Corridor and Historic West End?" From this very broad, ambiguous, and basic research question, there are several tangible research items expected. We expect the development of multidisciplinary cross-functional teams within and in concert with the university who will explore and investigate current literature to determine best practices for strength-based modeling and approaches. Once best practices are assessed, practitioners from the multidisciplinary cross-functional teams will teach, coach, and develop university faculty in their understanding of strength-based modeling and approaches. From this understanding and in support of JCSU's Quality Enhancement Plan, "Creating a culture of research," faculty will develop unambiguous research questions and hypotheses that investigate strength-based modeling and approaches to determine the effects on black men in the Northwest Corridor and Historic West End.

Field education, also known as a field practicum or field internship, is an important component of all Master of Social Work programs. Field placements are designed to enable graduate students to gain experience working in health services agencies while under the close supervision of field instructors. It is our hope and expectation that our investigative research will result in collaborations with health service agencies and our local government in proposed longitudinal studies for the JCSU Masters of Social Work program that supports field work components in that discipline coupled with the development of practitioner/faculty-mentored research activities for both undergraduate and graduate students. The benefits of this type of study is that we, as researchers, will be able to detect development or changes in characteristics of our target population at both the group and individual level. The key to this is to provide an examination that extends beyond a single moment in time, rather to establish a sequence of events. Perhaps, ambitiously, we hope to engage and impact our global community through our published works.

It is my hope that after reading these narratives and reflecting on each story, the book has brought about a clarity of vision, enlightened awareness, and deeper understanding despite the complex, hard issues requiring resolution. Community leaders, with candid conversations and brutal honesty, will be demonstrative of how they will utilize their networks and social capital to engage and assemble other black men, both young and old, who are willing to help make lives better for all who live in the Corridor.

Dr. Diane Bowles is vice president for Government Sponsored Programs at Johnson C. Smith University, and executive director of the Smith Institute for Applied Research.

ABOUT THE EDITOR

 Award-winning journalist **Ron Stodghill** has worked for *The New York Times, Time, Business Week,* and *Savoy,* for which he was editor in chief. An assistant professor in Interdisciplinary Studies at JCSU, Stodghill is the author of *Where Everybody Looks Like Me: At the Crossroads of America's Black Colleges and Culture* (HarperCollins/ Amistad). Stodghill also edited JCSU's anthology *Let There Be Light: Exploring How Charlotte's Historic West End is Shaping a New South.*